THE LIGHT OF AWARENESS

THE LIGHT OF AWARENESS

Ways and Means to Fullness of Life

John Graham

The Light of Awareness
Published and distributed by
John Gray Books
39 Moorland Road, Langho, Blackburn, BB6 8HA

Copyright 2001 John Graham Hindle
who asserts the right to the
nom-de-plume 'John Graham'

ISBN 0-9534609-4-0

British Library Cataloguing in Publication Data:
a catalogue record for this book is available from the
British library

Production, typesetting, printing and binding:
Proprint, Riverside Cottage, Great North Road,
Stibbington, Peterborough, PE8 6LR

PEOPLE TRAVEL TO WONDER
AT THE HEIGHT OF THE
  MOUNTAINS
AT THE HUGE WAVES OF
  THE SEA,
AT THE LONG COURSES
  OF RIVERS
AT THE VAST COMPASS
  OF THE OCEANS
AT THE CIRCULAR
  MOTIONS OF THE
  STARS
AND
THEY PASS THEMSELVES
  BY
WITHOUT WONDERING.

   St. Augustine.

'In order that the mind
should see the light
instead of darkness, so
the entire soul must be
turned away from this
changing world, until its
eye can learn to
contemplate reality and
that supreme splendour
which we have called the
Good. Hence there may well
be an art, whose aim would
be to effect this very
thing'.

   Socrates.

To my family - Babs for her courage and loyalty,
Alyson for her wisdom and humour
Sue for her enthusiasm and generosity.

PREFACE

The reader will become aware of certain themes or strands running through this book.

One is that we have become so pre-occupied with the mundane business of living, that we can not see the spiritual wood for the trees. Yet unless we do so, the outlook is bleak. For we fail to realise the potential life and joy which could be ours: we are in effect blind. Or asleep and oblivious to what could be.

Second, that the ability lies within us to recover our spiritual roots, to 'plug in' to our Source.

Third, the unoriginal phrase 'them that have eyes to see' keeps recurring. The paradox is that until we have realised our need and taken the first few steps, we may not be aware of what we have been missing.

Fourth, the central theme is probably 'The Means exist' - to wake up from automatic, robotic, everyday consciousness, reconnect with our Spirituality, and become aware of Life rather than mere existence.

The book also attempts to be pragmatic by including a section on 'Ways and Means', to enable and empower the seeker to discover and develop the rich resources within each of us.

It is for those who are disillusioned by religion and unfulfilled by materialism.

CONTENTS

INTRODUCTION

This book arose from a life-long need and attempt to make some sort of sense of it all. I have searched for wisdom and peace long and hard and in many spheres. I have struggled with learned and in-depth studies. I have digested tomes that were meant to be definitive philosophies, the Truth about Life. Most of them left me relatively cold and unsatisfied, although a few promised to inspire and kindle my Spirit.

However, I discarded none of them totally, because all contained elements of Truth. The hope therefore is that this breadth of collective knowledge and experience can lead to some sort of synthesis, a meaningful whole, to a semblance of Sense. If that sense is more emotional than intellectual, so be it.

I am aware that the book may be seen as somewhat presumptious, but I hope that it may also be regarded as brave in its attempt to fashion an outlook which is broad, positive and compassionate. It was probably written for my spiritual benefit; if others gain from it, that is a bonus and a blessing. Any slight Christian bias due to my upbringing is by no means orthodox.

I must admit to a long-time fascination with psychology - but with two provisos, a) it ought to be useful and valuable to humanity and b) it ought to enhance every aspect of our living, including Spirituality. I am not interested in the Freudian-type approach which concentrates on psycho-pathology: it might not be necessary if we embraced the approaches of Maslow and Perls and their belief in the Human potential for health and Wholeness, in effect a psychology of the spirit.

What I believe I have found is the Wholeness of everything; a philosophy which embraces not only psychology but also the natural sciences and many of the great religious concepts of the world.

Like most people, I have had no great insights or revelations, nor am I particularly mystical, though with one exception. As a teenager, when sat in church one evening in the atmosphere of a rather beautiful Harvest Festival, I had a brief sense of the perfection behind everything. It was as if I was looking beyond time and space and just knew that this existence is a poor reflection of an underlying harmony and that all will be well in the end. I have never been able to recover those fleeting moments but neither can I ignore them. For long I told no-one about this, until I came across the following extract and realised I was not alone:

'I know nothing of the ecstacy of the mystics, except for one illuminating personal experience. A flash of insight not induced by first love, religious fervour or mental or spiritual auto-intoxication. Nor was it drug-induced. Unsought, surprising - a split-second of time; not so much a vision of beauty or harmony, but the certain knowledge that they existed. The briefest moment, yet so illuminating and life-giving, that it still seems more vivid than all the days and years of my life.

The best description I can give is that it was a marriage of the mind with the universal mind (whatever that is) - satisfying and complete... A man fortunate enough to have had such an experience could never go down to his grave with bitterness, for he has tasted, and what is more important knows that he has tasted, the height and depth of the fullness of life'.

from 'The Imprisoned Splendour' by Raynor C. Johnson

I have since discovered that many people have had similar experiences.

I have also experienced some precious moments whilst sampling some of the 'Ways and Means' referred to in these pages. Maybe I am a romantic but I know of a number of hard-boiled people who have been deeply affected and influenced for the better by these means. It is a case of finding the Way which suits you. I suspect that all routes lead to the same goal, indicating that our diversity leads to eventual Unity.

The following extract appeals to me as a very pragmatic view of Spirituality:

'It always surprises me when people ask about my religion. Healers and mediums belong to all sorts of religions, but healing is a beautiful spiritual experience. To me there is an important distinction. Religion is a man-made concept, with sets of rules based on the Bible or other religious books. Spirituality is your spontaneous reaction to life; if you are a loving and compassionate

person, you won't need rules to stop you from doing wrong or harmful actions; you simply won't want to.

Truly spiritual people are those who have lived and learned through many lifetimes, and have acquired love and compassion as their minds have expanded. There are levels and degrees of spirituality, according to how far your mind has progressed. Spiritually progressed people do not need to be guided by religious dogma; in fact I find that they have a code of honour and a tolerance that I don't often see practiced by some people who regard themselves as religious'.

from 'Mind to Mind' by Betty Shine.

The Resource Directory is obviously an integral part of the book, backing up the frequent assertions that 'The Means Exist'.

This little book is probably best used by 'delving'. It is not intended to think for you, but perhaps to stimulate thought and - dare I hope - enhance awareness.

The intention is to reassure, stimulate and encourage exploration, because I believe that not only do we have the means to realise the potential within us, as individuals and as a race, but that everything we need is provided; never more so than in this enlightened age. The change must always start in the heart of the individual.

John Graham
December 2000

REFLECTIONS

ALLEGORY

'Imagine people chained up inside a dark, underground cave. A fire burns at the entrance, and in its flickering light, shadows of the outside world are projected onto the walls of the cave. The prisoners, immobilised by their chains, can see nothing but these shadows of reality. One day, one of the captives is liberated and dragged out of the cave. At first he is blinded by the sunlight, but as his vision clears, he is stunned to realise that this is the magnificent real world, that the shadows on the wall are mere illusions. The man rushes back to inform the others - but they laugh at his crazy tales of the 'real world' and cling relentlessly to their chains'.

Plato.

COMING ALIVE

Down the ages, wise people of many cultures have insisted that Human Beings are asleep. In a dream, we live out our lives as robots, blind to the hidden truths of the Universe, which are there for those who seek.

Without insight into Reality; no awareness of the truths behind the glittering illusions of life. No appreciation that the 'real' world is fantasy - or virtual reality.

How can this be, when life is getting faster and human beings cleverer, cramming more and more into life, apparently getting more and more out of it. Becoming ever more satisfied and fulfilled.

Why, then, is there so much stress, escapism, crime, murder, suicide, self-abuse and seeking after the next thrill or trend? As well as poisoning the world and squandering resources.

Because we are not asking the right questions (if we are seeking at all), not looking in the right places, not realising what we are missing - or have lost.

Such as insight, intuition, sensitivity, beauty, quality, truth, peace, joy, wisdom, magic, miracles and light.

To summarise the words of one of the great Teachers of history, how do we benefit if we gain the whole world, only to lose our Soul and pass through life like blind people? He also said 'Seek and you shall find, ask and you shall receive, knock and it shall be opened to you'.

'The human race is in virtual mutiny to the order of the Universe'

Buzz Aldrin, Astronaut.

SELF-AWARENESS

If most human beings are asleep, living on an automatic level without insight, the consequences for individuals and for the world are worrying to say the least.

Programmed by our upbringing and the limitations and prejudices of our parents, ancestors and culture, we perpetuate old beliefs and habit patterns, often learned before we developed a critical faculty and operating beneath the conscious level. In this sense there is a similarity to the animals, products of instinct and survival techniques imitated from parents and peers. Living in continual fear, not knowing why they do what they do. A quality of life which leaves much to be desired.

Thus with most human beings, at an appropriate stimulus the old habitual behavioural tape-loop switches on and we act without thinking, often in an insensitive way, which does us no favours and often aggravates the world's troubles.

Those who can consciously interfere with this process come Alive. They become the players, not the pawns, truly in control of what they become. Able to influence and enhance Life.

But first we must gain insight and awareness into ourselves.

'I believe that sensitivity to love and beauty are inherent qualities that come naturally with human beingness.

I further believe that these qualities would be far more universal and apparent, was it not for the truth that each generation of human youth have been taught to accept, even emulate, the insensitivities and barbarisms of their forefathers'.

Tim Daly.

SENSITIVITY

We are all neurotic, to varying degree, simply because we are alive. To be alive means to be sensitive to our environment. Irritability, in the sense of tendency to respond/react, is a defining characteristic of the nervous system and we are all as good as our nervous system allows. Sensitivity is a characteristic of life and those in whom it is diminished are either half dead or dangerous.

Neuroticism accrues from avoiding the pain of growing up. Understandable and forgiveable as this may be, we do ourselves no favours in the long run. We end up either pulling up the drawbridge or manipulating others, rather than taking reponsibility for ourselves.

As babies, we are sensitive and vulnerable. Along the way, life experiences toughen us, or at least form a hard protective shell. As adults we learn to cope somehow by developing defence mechanisms, but hide what is going on inside.

Thus millions of adults live out their lives in their hard shells, in fear and mistrust, hardly daring to reveal themselves. Yet only by such disclosure can they begin to truly Live, to give and receive, to develop their inner Selves, and start to realise their potential as fully aware human beings.

To be what we were created to be. The means have never been more available if we truly seek.

'If you're suffering, you're asleep. Do you want a sign that you're asleep? Here it is: You're suffering'.

Anthony de Mello, 'Awareness'.

INSECURITY

Most of the world's troubles are born of vulnerability; most 'sins' are a consequence of our insecurity. For both breed fear, which leads to defensiveness, aggression, hate and prejudice.

But how, when we are born naked and helpless into a world of change, frustration and uncertainty, do we avoid this vicious, negative circle.

By seeking the means to grow up with and stay in touch with the natural laws of the Universe, the rhythms of life, the Wisdom of the Ancients; by cultivating intuition and Spirituality. It is never too late.

By doing so, we can recover and retain our original sensitivity, the insight which is essential for effective relationships with others, with nature, with the Divine.

Only when we are thus reconnected to our Spiritual source will we know the Joy of being in touch - in every sense - centred, grounded, secure.

'Deep within the human soul lies an unfamiliar force which is stronger than all external forces that surround us. The force is unfamiliar because we have forgotten what it sounds like and what it needs to release it.'

HRH The Prince of Wales.

SIN

We are all born helpless, weak, dependent, sensitive and vulnerable. We are created individual and alone, with powerful needs and drives. Is it any wonder that people go wrong, or become prejudiced, bitter or hard?

The Human mind is a delicate, sensitive, mysterious and amazing mechanism. As the old Testament puts it, 'We are fearfully and wonderfully made'.

Perhaps the marvel is that some people do become reasonably mature and creative in these circumstances.

The Concept of Sin has been used and abused to fill people's hearts with guilt and fear, leaving no room for love and joy, which can never co-exist with fear

From further along the Path, most Sin is likely to be forgiveable, because it is committed from an imperfect and inadequate viewpoint.

Except possibly that of turning our backs on the Light: wilful Spiritual blindness.

'Our Higher Self, which loves us unconditionally, yearns for us to learn and grow - and if we refuse to grow through Joy, it will reluctantly send us struggle. If we ignore the carrot of our 'dreams', then we invite the 'stick' of struggle.

from 'Dreaming the Dark'.

THE NEED (1)

Human beings can understand everything but themselves.

We develop a more and more complex lifestyle. One invention follows and complicates another, without a thought as to their cumulative effect on society; then we wonder why we commit the most heinous acts against each other at an accelerating rate. The world's misery seems to increase exponentially.

We are clever but not wise. We lack, or have lost, insight and sensitivity. Other eras and cultures were wiser, but we sneer at them. We have concentrated on the external rather than the internal. We have developed our left brain at the expense of the right. We have lost touch with the innate wisdom, guidance, spirituality and morality within us.

The good news is that it is still there, waiting to be tapped. The Divine spark, though dormant, is ready to be re-kindled and our only hope is that we re-discover the skills to do so.

Most of the world's misery is due to vulnerability, insecurity, isolation and consequent fear and frustration. Only when we develop the sensitivity and charity to realise this will we help ourselves and others. Only when we realise, with joy, that we are intended to be an integral part of nature and the Divine will we throw off our burden of ignorance and depression.

'Those wise ones who see that the consciousness within themselves is the same within all conscious beings attain eternal peace'

Katha Upanishad

TRANSCENDENCE AND IMMANENCE

Balancing the doctrine of original sin, there must be a doctrine of original blessing. The former assumes we are abject miserable sinners separated from a majestic, distant, transcendental God, approachable only via blood sacrifice or intermediary.

Of course there is some truth in this. In the main we have temporarily lost the art and gift of recognising and responding to the Spiritual.

Original blessing implies that we are in fact children of the Divine, with a distant memory of and a longing for our source and our home. That birthright will always be ours.

The Divine is not only high, mighty, rational, theoretical and transcendent but also integral, intimate, intuitive, practical and immanent.

The trouble is, humanity tries to identify primarily with a transcendent God, succeeding only in being detached, authoritarian and arrogant, thus creating the world we have.

In practice all that we can really identify with on this material plane is the Immanent. In essence, this means that the Divine is not only manifest in many ways in this world, macrocosm and microcosm, it can also be directly appreciated by the Divine in us and every other being and creature, for 'the Kingdom of Heaven is within you'.

But a mirror needs to be oriented in the direction of the sun to reflect its brilliance

'Another form of consciousness is possible. Indeed, it has existed from earliest times, underlies other cultures and has survived even in the West in hidden streams. This is the consciousness I call Immanent - the awareness of the world and everything in it as alive, dynamic, interdependent, interacting, and infused with moving energies: a living being, a weaving dance.'

from 'Dreaming the Dark'.

SUPERNATURAL

Many people refuse to give credence to the supernatural, the ethereal, the spiritual. They credit only what they can see, hear, taste, touch, smell. But there are extra-sensory experiences which are at least as valid. Not only are the senses limited and changeable, but they can be distorted and fooled.

Beneath the material illusion of reality, at the molecular level, there is only space and energy. At this level, there are varying degrees of stability. On our every day level, change is the norm. Everything is arbitrary and there are few absolutes. Not only that but human beings are so fragile. How can anything so transient as life be real. Surely we are the ghosts.

We flit through life half awake. Few of can us savour and appreciate every waking moment.

Life is an allegory and a paradox. The visible, the material, the apparent, is a pale reflection of, an indicator of, a clue to the Real which lies just beyond the obvious and is perceived by developing more subtle means, activating latent intuitive sensors and abilities.

Paradoxically, the Real can only be apprehended by the apparently invisible i.e. the intuition and sensitivity at humanity's core. But the conditions must be created for this, such as humility, honesty, and the cultivation of a 'wise innocence'. We must become 'as little children' if we want to see the Kingdom of Heaven which has always been within us.

In other words, turn our faces from the obvious to the Truth.

'Don't seek the truth......just drop your opinions'.

Japanese Zen Master.

RELIGION

Despite its failings, there still seems to be a world-wide need for religion. We still, deep down, crave a 're-joining' with our source, the Divine, the Cosmic or what you will.

Unfortunately, people try to trivialise God, to package and dogmatise Him/Her. To make out that He/She is partisan. It is no surprise that our small minds make God too small.

Religion, or the spiritual appetite, needs a shift of focus. From an external, detached, dreaded God, to see God in Man. Fear, in the sense of apprehension and anxiety, needs to be removed from religion, to be replaced by compassion between people (in the bible, 'fear' is used in the sense of respect). If God is Love, then fear and love are incompatible.

We need to still our silly little minds and allow the Divine to shine through. It is there waiting for us to be kind to ourselves. Then we will see Him in ourselves and others. We are, or could be, the expression of the Divine.

That must start with self-respect; ironically, we have too much Ego and not enough self-esteem. Then we must get rid of the notion that we are abject sinners, currying favour with a wrathful distant God.

If we paid half as much attention to human beings as we pay lip-service to an external God, He/She would not only be worshipped but well-pleased. We might even begin to make in-roads into the mess we are in. The place to start is ourselves

Doing so may enable us to see through our differences, to those things which unite us as manifestations of the Divine.

'Like the bee gathering honey from the flowers, the wise man accepts the essence of different scriptures and sees only the good in all religion'.

Srimad Bhagavatam

SPIRITUALITY

The concept of Spirituality is not easy to define, yet perhaps easily recognised. It is anything which causes our spirit to kindle, to come alive, to grow, to soar, to sing; via a means which is either permanent or cumulative, and which does not enslave or bypass personal responsibility. It is anything which causes us to love Life, to wonder, to be humble, to be grateful, to be joyful, and to want to share the benefits.

The opposites of Spirituality, of being fully aware, of being truly alive, are dormancy, deterioration and death.

We can choose to go one way or the other - either to stagnate (or rather deteriorate, for it is impossible to stand still), or to embrace the rare chance to put our feet on the road to Spirituality and thus realise the latent spark of Divinity within each of us.

Through an open but not gullible mind, a heart that allows itself to be just a little romantic and adventurous, and a will that shows humility, courage and a certain faith, magic and miracles will guide us to unexpected Spiritual fruits, and our Divine goal - Peace, truth, Wisdom, Joy and Love.

'Are you a God? they asked the Buddha. No, he replied.
Are you an angel then? No.
A saint? No.
Then what are you?
Replied the Buddha, I am awake'.

ILLUSION AND REALITY

The boundaries of illusion and reality are becoming blurred, in fact have done so.

We seek diversion from the everyday world because we perceive it as ugly, boring, monotonous or simply painful. These things obscure the fact that it can also be fascinating, rewarding and joyful.

Not only do people regard soap operas, the stars and their lifestyles as real and desirable but we seek every opportunity to escape, whether into drugs of all descriptions or into virtual reality. We worship our cars and possessions or think that football is more important than life.

Throughout the Gospels, Jesus emphasised the falseness of the material ('Lay not up for yourselves treasure upon earth').

If people of his time had trouble distinguishing the spiritually real from the materially false, we have less chance.

A fascinating world, when kept in perspective, has become only too enthralling. Sadly we are literally 'in thrall', subservient to whatever entity in whose interests it is to preserve our blindness, if you hypothesise a Devil. Or simply to our lower sightless nature.

'A lion encountered a flock of sheep and to his great surprise found a lion amongst them. It was a lion who had been raised by the sheep since he was a cub, copying their movements and their bleat. The lion went straight for him, and when the sheep/lion looked at the real one, he started to quake. The lion said to him, 'What are you doing among these sheep?' And the sheep/lion said 'I am a sheep'. And the lion said, 'Nonsense!. Follow me'. He took the sheep/lion to a pool and said, 'What do you see?' When the sheep/lionsaw his image in the water, he gave a great roar. From that day, he was changed forever'.

Anonymous

19

WHEN WILL WE SEE

The world appears to be in accelerating chaos. The trigger factors include excessive stimulus, hyperactivity, misuse of energy, competition, and unbridled technology.

Apparent alone-ness and pointlessness cause us to seek to forget by throwing ourselves into ever-increasing activity, thankful for technologies such as hydrocarbons and electronics which enable us to do so.

We are mesmerised and en-thralled by the apparent glitter and sophistication of the world. The consequence is ever-increasing blindness, indifference, insensitivity and the outcomes thereof.

We all strive to be happy and it has been observed that most crime is this striving carried to excess. We need to learn to stop striving.

We move further and further from our birthright of naturalness, insight, intuition, humanity and relationship with the cosmic and the divine.

Stopping the rot is possible, given the will and the heart. The means are there for all.

....to find the universal elements enough; to find the air and the water exhilarating; to be refreshed by a morning walk or an evening saunter....to be thrilled by the stars at night; to be elated over a birds nest or a wild flower in spring - these are some of the rewards of the simple life'.

John Burrows.

MORALITY, LOVE AND RELIGION

Surely evil, scheming, devious humanity needs the big stick - the promise of judgement and the wrath of God. The hard line may be the only answer against those whose upbringing has resulted in criminal or psychopathic tendencies.

However, the big stick doesn't even work very well on the human level. It produces either unthinking sullen conformity and/or resentment, revenge and violence. Such conformity can never be permanent, except that these negative attitudes are passed on to each generation, contributing to global insensitivity. It also stifles so much creativity, compassion and humanity; that can not be moral.

The only morality worth having is that which is internalised, that which is second nature and which we feel, based on such ethics as Do As You Would Be Done By and Fellow Feeling Makes Us Wondrous Kind. Even this arises from selfishess - but at least it is likely to be sensitive and spontaneous. The doctrine of Love thy Neighbour is not intellectual; it must come from the heart. Parental love is also powerful, in that it may sacrifice whether merited or not; but that tends to come from the gut, almost as a reflex.

In another dimension is altruistic love, the kind that aches to heal the whole of humanity. But that is hard to practice because you can not embrace the whole human race and it may mean caring but not interfering.

'Religion is a man-made concept, with sets of rules based on the Bible or other religious book. Spirituality is your spontaneous reaction to life; if you are a loving and compassionate person, you won't need rules to stop you from doing wrong or harmful actions: you simply won't want to'.

Betty Shine, from 'Mind to Mind'.

WHY?

Misfortune occurs daily; crashes of all kinds, illness, fires, drowning. In despair, we cry, 'Why does God allow it?'

In more rational moments, we may realise that in a technological world there will be failures, whether due to materials, engineering, poor maintenance or human error. Calculated risks will not always work out, and God is not a factor. Even personal accident is often down to lack of judgement, skill or a troubled mind which clouds our observation and concentration.

Of course, natural phenomena such as weather can increase the obstacles and risk, but these are hardly personal or vindictive. Just the act of living and having to participate puts us at risk; we can not exist in a cocoon.

What of famine, flood and pestilence? Again we are perhaps 50% to blame. We build dwellings on flood planes. We contribute to the cause of some diseases. Half the world starves because we do not consider people important; we treat them as cannon fodder or as a resource to be exploited or discarded.

However there are still the X-factors of natural disaster, disease and deterioration. At present we can only speculate on why, although there is evidence that if we develop the right attitude then health and aging problems may be ameliorated.

However God is the supreme magician as well as the supreme scientist. He can turn water into wine, restore the sick to health and miraculously resurrect and illuminate our dormant souls. Therefore we can have quiet confidence that ultimately all will be well; the loose strands of our existence will gathered into the tapestry of life.

'O Joy that seekest me through pain,
I can not close my heart to thee;
I trace the rainbow through the rain,
And feel the promise is not vain,
That morn shall tearless be.'
George Matheson

EVIL

Sadly it must be acknowledged that there is real evil in this world. Or at least people who are largely evil, although even they may be good to their mothers.

You can argue nature/nurture ad infinitum (which is akin to trying to measure the area of a field without knowing one or both dimensions). But undoubtedly there are people who are nasty from an early age and seem to get beyond the possibility of change.

Perhaps they may change through more than one life. Perhaps they exist to provide a benchmark by which the rest of us can measure ourselves.

Of course there is the possibility that fate sends each of us into the world to play a role in the drama of life, but that does not alter the fact that there are certain people who exhibit evil tendencies.

We need to learn to recognise them and avoid them. It has been said that they should be put on an island and left to evolve their own society.

But the problem needs to be seen in perspective. Just as there are very few really good people, there are also very few who come into the really bad category. The majority are either decent or capable of change in the right milieu. To deny this is to write off so much human potential.

No doubt all will one day be revealed.

'For now we see through a glass darkly, but then face to face. Now I know in part, but then I shall know even as I also am known'.

St. Paul, The New Testament.

THE INFLUENCE OF EVIL

Logically of course there isn't a Devil or any such force. But if one is hypothesised, then ways become apparent in which 'he' desensitises and enslaves us.

* Insecurity and feelings of aloneness and separateness.

* Superstition and fear. Our apparent isolation and insignificance in the Universe.

* Lack of a sense of purpose and feeling valued.

* Rivalry, winning, competition, one-upmanship. Also includes taunting, teasing, put-downs, mocking, if done to feed our egotism and insecurity (i.e. to score points and feel good at someone elses expense.)

* Money - as be-all and end-all. Leading to the rat-race and world empires of commercialism

* Pre-occupation with clever technology and its insensitive and arrogant use.

* Excessive diversion and escape from reality, by chemical and electronic means.

* Boredom and loss of sense of wonder. Loss of proportion and healthy humility.

* Obsessions, compulsions, the need to possess, control, dominate.

* Bedazzlement by the material, the visual, the concrete, the powerful.

* Pride beyond simple joy.

'The only devils in this world are those running around in our own hearts; that is where all our battles should be fought'.

Mahatma Ghandi.

PAIN

In a practical sense, pain is a warning. A stomach pain may be appendicitis, which can kill. Pain is also a teacher, saving us if we heed its lesson; hot things can burn, falling can damage us.

Pain can also be a spur and a stimulus, for 'No pain, no gain'. However everybody's pain threshold differs.

If others cause us pain, it can evoke retaliation and conflict which needs resolution. So primitively it can be the basis of social living, establishing the principal of 'do as you would be done by'. Psychological pain also in relationships can be a steep learning curve, causing us to choose friends and partners wisely.

However life is not intended to be excessively painful. Apart from the phenomenon of masochism, too much pain can screw us up, diminishing joy and leading to anger, depression, bitterness and despair.

For long now there has been emphasis on toughness and endurance. Anything carried to excess is unbalanced and dangerous. Bravery is not always the virtue it is made out be. We are often brave as a reflex response or because we would not be able to live with ourselves or others. Bravery may be down to group bravado, or because we fear a coward's reputation - or simply down to the effects of hormones.

Human beings are created exquisitely sensitive and that makes them pathetically vulnerable. We need some self-discipline, but not at all costs and not at the expense of our humanity and spirituality.

In the few cases where pain becomes chronic, intolerable and untreatable and there is no chance of recovery of viability and a life with quality, then dignity demands an end, if it is chosen rationally

Although we can be forgiven the paranoia at times of thinking that pain is malevolent and vindictive, it can fulfill an essential purpose. However perhaps only now that we have the means to largely control it can we rationalise about pain in this way.

'Pain is the breaking of the shell which surrounds your understanding'.

Kahlil Gibran, 'The Prophet'.

POINT AND PURPOSE (1)

'Call the world if you please "The Vale of Soul-making". Then you will find out the best use of the world......I say 'soul-making', soul as distinguished from an intelligence - there may be intelligence or sparks of the divinity in millions - but they are not souls till they acquire identities, till each one is personally itself. I(n)telligences are atoms of perception - they know and they see and they are pure, in short they are God - How then are souls to be made? How then are these sparks which are God to have identity given them - so as ever to possess a bliss peculiar to each ones individual existence? How but by the medium of a world like this?.....I will call the world a school instituted for the purpose of teaching little children to read - I will call the human heart the .....book used in that school - and I will call the child able to read the Soul made from that school and its book.

Do you not see how necessary a world of pains and troubles is to school an intelligence and make it a soul? A place where the heart must feel and suffer in a thousand diverse ways......as various as the lives of men are - so various become their souls and thus does God make individual beings, Souls, Identical Souls of the sparks of his own essence - This appears to me a faint sketch of a system of salvation which does not affront our reason and humanity'.

Letter from John Keats to his brother George, 21st April, 1819.

POINT AND PURPOSE (2)

Most of the selfishness and sin of humanity is down to two reasons:

1. We do not feel valued and

2. We feel no sense of purpose. We are adrift on a sea of life, if not without power then certainly without a rudder.

Most human beings are basically not evil. If we felt connected to our source and that life was leading somwhere, most people would not only co-operate with life instead of rebelling; they would respond positively, even joyfully.

If we knew where we had come from and where we were going, it would be a tremendous relief; the world would be transformed in spite of its differences. The answer lies in raising our awareness levels i.e. a heightened awareness of the marvel of life and a sensitivity to our true spiritual nature, which is indestructible.

Then we would know we had worth. Then we would know without a shadow of doubt that our purpose is to explore, experience and know all aspects of self on our journey to the place from which we came.

And we would do it willingly for we would be certain that all would indeed be well.

'Shining the light of awareness into our fears is often all that is necessary to dispell the shadows'

from 'Stepping into the Magic'

DOGMA AND DESTINY

These days, those who dogmatise get short shrift. People demand the right to their own opinions.

You would think that science was bringing us nearer and nearer to objective Truth, to ultimate answers which we could proclaim without a shadow of a doubt, thus uniting us all in our cleverness.

Yet scientists now find there are few if any absolutes. Paradoxically, everything has another aspect, which can exist at one and the same time - for those who can perceive it, for the eye of the observer must come into every equation. The wise must always keep an open mind, so where is the certainty we crave?

People feel lost without something solid and permanent to grasp. And this human insecurity leads to much of the 'sin' in this world. We might be able to relax in our human-ness if we saw or felt that there was point and purpose in life, a Plan, a goal, a benevolent aim. That might mean that, however insignificant we appear in the scheme of things, our life and our efforts would not be wasted. Most of us would respond to a sense of purpose and logic.

There is no one way: we must find our own, by seeking and discovering the resources which were implanted in us from the beginning. At times we may need a little help, but it is widely available.

Only in the last few decades has the realization dawned that we are not the pawns in the game but the players, or at least Partners in the Process.

Now, the truths of 'New Consciousness', based on age-old concepts, are available to all.

*'In order that the mind should see the light
instead of darkness, so the entire soul must be
turned away from this changing world, until its eye can learn to
contemplate reality and that supreme splendour
which we have called the Good. Hence there may well
be an art, whose aim would be to effect this very thing'.*

Socrates.

CHANGE

On our normal level, all life is change. It appears unpredictable, dissolving and reforming all the time.

On the one hand, this insecurity is worrying and depressing. On the other, it can be exciting and hopeful. Ironically, we live in a constant state of flux - possibly the only absolute apart from death, which itself is a form of change.

If the fact of change is disturbing, it may be as well to remember that nothing can ever be destroyed; it simply changes form.

Change may be challenging when we are young and have the resources to cope, but in the long term it is a source of anxiety, causing us to seek for something more permanent. We search for a stable relationship, then worry about it ending.

It makes sense therefore to try to determine if there is a more real world, a level or sphere of greater permanence. Or at least a philosophy or way which copes with the fact of change.

Many have found that this is so when they search with sincerity and an open mind.

'God's light dwells in the self and no-where else. It shines in every living being and one can see it with one's mind steadied.....if the world is what it is, it is because of tension. The world of time and change is ever striving to reach perfection'

Buddhist teaching.

OPPORTUNITY

At death, our development stage becomes fixed, like a photograph. Afterwards there can be no change, whether of deterioration or improvement, until another life. For only in life can we progress; only in life is change possible.

It is ironic and contrary, the existential dilemma that life matters, yet it doesn't, because it doesn't make sense. Everything matters, yet doesn't matter.

For while change is the norm and there is no certainty, the unpredictability can seem frightening.

However on the positive side, the odds mean as much joy as grief and uncertainty can be exciting. From the spiritual viewpoint it also implies hope.

For life is the only arena for progress, growth and improvement. Everyday we face choices which matter. Even one day can make a difference and perhaps we should remember the words of Queen Elizabeth 1 at the end of her life, 'All my possessions for a moment of time'.

'Teach me to care and not to care.
Teach me to be still'.
T.S. Eliot

PARTNERSHIP

It could all be so different - if we would bend our stiff necks, come off our high horses and stop trying to put it all right ourselves.

There is great healing power and energy just waiting to embrace us - if we will only allow it.

God does not want to be abjectly worshipped. (S)He does not want a relationship based on fear and inequality.

Of course 'He' is omnipotent, but we have been created with free will, with the individuality, freedom and power to choose to give ourselves back, to be re-united.

It is said that, insignificant as we seem, for this reason we are powerful spiritual beings. And it is true that in us now, and at every moment we are in this life, lies the power to veto or co-operate with the Universe.

Who would want to interfere with this potential for co-creation? To do so is probably the only definition of sin, which brings us back to the fact that the wages of sin is Spiritual separation from the Light.

'In a world which is rife with conflicts that cause enormous suffering, it is time we gain a deeper understanding of what is happening and develop the skills to co-create change'.

Ben Fuchs.

ALL WILL BE WELL (1)

Optimism in this poor, imperfect world is surely madness. Is it unrealistic to have hope, when all things are fragile and all things appear to end?

Only if we can see life as a transient but essential, invaluable experience and a pale reflection of a reality much greater, more wonderful and more permanent does it make sense.

In this context it falls into place. Human love and longing , the mystery and magnificence of the Universe, and all the dilemmas of our existence, gain significance from this viewpoint.

But to benefit from the potentially precious experience that is life, we need to cast away all pre-conceived concepts and, in humility, seek the means to reach the joy of our own inner nature, to be who we really are and were always meant to be.

Thus we may develop a more direct relationship with the Universe, and whatever higher forces govern our lives.

'Don't seek the Truth......just drop your opinions.'

Japanese Zen Master

ALL WILL BE WELL (2)

Life, depending on the outlook you developed/inherited and the deck of cards you were dealt, is a joyful experience, a magnificent tragedy or hell on earth.

It is a struggle for most of us but the road is more unequal for some than others.

Atheism is understandable in this short, hard life on this turbulent, damaged, lonely planet.

Yet there are many who have been privileged to see beyond the obvious and through the illusion.

Some have done so by believing this can not be all there is and determinedly seeking the Truth.

Others, like Einstein, have been brought to their knees finding God through science.

Some have come to the end of their resources and sought and found wisdom when they cried 'Please help me!'.

There are more gateways than one, given the will.

'When the student is ready, the teacher will come'.

Buddhist saying.

SEEING BEYOND

After the first flush of youth, after our early urges and drives are fulfilled, what then?

Many people become disillusioned and disatisfied and yearn for something more, something higher, something more permanent. They come to the realisation that material alone can not satisfy our soul and spirit.

We need a higher aspiration. An increasing number of fortunate souls have taken the steps to create conducive conditions to achieve the breakthrough. They literally 'see the Light'.

They seem to function on a different level, with a new vision. Their guiding light comes from within, from heightened senses and a new sense of self, enabling them to perceive the world in a different and rarified light.

Acknowledge the Light. The Light within. The light above and beyond.

This territory/plane/sphere - the ostensible world - is symbolic, an imitation, a representation. But it can also be a clue, a promise, a sign; giving hope, fuelling our yearning.

'I know nothing of the ecstacy of the mystics, except for one illuminating personal experience. A flash of insight not induced by first love, religious fervour or mental or spiritual auto-intoxication. Unsought, surprising - a split-second of time; not so much a vision of beauty or harmony, but the certain knowledge that they existed. The briefest moment, yet so illuminating and life-giving, that it still seems more vivid than all the days and years of my life.

The best description I can give is that it was a marriage of the mind with the universal mind, satisfying and complete....... A man fortunate enough to have had such an experience could never go down to his grave with bitterness for he has tasted, and what is more important knows that he has tasted, the height and depth of the fullness of life'.

from 'The Imprisoned Splendour' by Raynor C. Johnson

CONSCIOUSNESS

There is a view which says the mind is organised vertically or hierarchically, into various conscious and sub-conscious strata; and the evidence for levels beyond the conscious is strong. For inspiration does not normally spring from the rational, logical mind.

However recent research points to the brain-mind being more complex, showing a distinct lateral split. The left hemisphere deals with logic, numeracy and language. It concerns itself with parts and details, operating in linear fashion step by step; it is in this sense blind, because the end result is not immediately obvious.

As these aspects of mind have been allowed to dominate in recent centuries, no wonder the world is in the dark.

The right brain on the other hand, is more intuitive, artistic and imaginative, concerning itself with patterns and wholes and expressing itself symbolically as in dreams. It may know without knowing how it knows.

Although we are all different, in recent centuries, the rational, logical, 'masculine' has been emphasised at the expense of the intuitive, and 'feminine'. They are meant to supplement each other, working as an integrated whole.

To make an exquisite piece of furniture, the craftsman needs artistry and practicality. To discover the Theory of Relativity, Einstein needed first to visualise or dream the possibilty: the equations came later.

'Eastern mystical traditions have always regarded consciousness as an integral part of the Universe. In the Eastern view, human beings, like all other life forms, are parts of an inseparable organic whole. Their intelligence therefore implies that the whole too is intelligent.

Human beings are seen as the living proof of cosmic intelligence; in us, the Universe repeats over and over again, its ability to produce forms through which it becomes consciously aware of itself.'

Fritz Capra, The Tao of Physics.

THOUGHT

Before it learns to think, the infant is simply aware, absorbing information via the senses i.e. perceiving the world.

Then formal learning occurs. Naming and labelling, analysing and categorising, we organise or pigeon-hole percepts into concepts, which are collections of related ideas, forming symbols or maps of reality. Their advantage is that they facilitate everyday living.

But they are not reality; they are second-hand representations of the world. Therefore in a sense we live in an unreal world, a world of illusion.

The process of thinking distances us from contact with life and many of our activities and institutions are substitutes for real living. They get in the way of immediate sensory, emotional and spiritual experience. It is possible to live so much in our mind that we lose touch with other aspects of our personality.

Only by recognising the fact and jettisoning the illusions of our mind can we become real again, recovering the mind of the child with the experience and wisdom of the adult.

'Are you imprisoned by your concepts?. Do you want to break out of your prison? Then look; observe; spend hours observing. Watching what? Anything. The faces of people, the shapes of trees, a bird in flight, a pile of stones, watch the grass grow. Get in touch with things, look at them. Hopefully, you will then break out of those rigid patterns we have all developed, out of what our thoughts and words have imposed on us'.

Anthony de Mello, 'Awareness'.

MIND

To put mind in context, it is an aspect of personality, together with body, emotions and spirit. It has its role and purpose but is not meant to dominate. It is best regarded as a tool, or an energy like electricity, to be activated when appropriate and turned off as necessary. There is a time for logic, but not at the expense of sensation, feeling, imagination, inspiration and the many other aspects of personality.

Mind should not be underestimated. Give it enthusiasm and direction and watch it go - terrier-like it pursues its goal almost obsessively as if with tunnel-vision. Ironically, in a sense it is mindless.

Because mental activity has been prized and developed at the expense of other facets and talents, much human activity resembles this frenetic, blinkered behaviour. The consequent world-picture can be frightening and depressing.

Positive thought can be an invaluable ally, but negative or undisciplined mental activity can be extremely damaging. It may be that God can only work with positive thought.

When Mind is seen in context as only part of our make-up, a good servant but a bad master, the need to take steps to put it in its place in the scheme of things becomes apparent. It needs control but paradoxically this is achieved not by an act of will, but by turning off and letting go - putting the mind out of gear.

'Nothing is good or bad, but thinking makes it so'.

Shakespeare.

HOW THOUGHT DIVIDES

We are granted the gift and power of a degree of independent thought and we abuse it. Our little thoughts run away with us and take over, chattering round our head like the Buddhist 'monkey-mind'. Not until we realise the situation and long to still our undisciplined minds have we a chance of peace. Our minds are an obstacle to progress in personal and spiritual development, which is why the Bible exhorts us to 'Be still and know that I am God'.

There is an awful inevitability in the process of the way our minds take the world apart. Instead of using them under strict control as a useful tool in the business of living, without thinking we allow them to divide and destroy.

We compare and contrast. We weigh and balance. We analyse. We judge. We form opinions. We develop prejudices. We argue. We accuse. We divide. We hate. We cause strife, war, damage, death. The mind is a good servant but a bad master.

'Strict control' does not mean concentration and discipline: rather the opposite. It means relaxation i.e. putting the mind out of gear when appropriate, thus allowing other aspects of consciousness such as sensation, feeling and imagery, to come to the fore. It means putting thought in its place. In the context of higher consciousness.

If we seek the means to become aware of the dangers and to put the power of thought into perspective, there is a chance of non-judgement, acceptance, harmony, unity, love, peace; and all consequent blessings.

'The mind creates chasms.....the heart can build bridges'

Anonymous

CONDITIONING

We are very much creatures of habit: we repeat those behaviours that have had some pay-off for us. We become stuck in behavioural loops, because it makes life simpler. Particularly in early life, we pick up prejudices, often unthinkingly, which are thus perpetuated from generation to generation. They are fed by our vulnerability, insecurity and fear.

At best such faulty attitudes are narrow and unhelpful, at worst dangerous and disastrous in their effects.

If only we could stand back and take a fresh, new look at ourselves, as with the Buddhist 'Beginners mind', and realise that it is selves like us who make the world what it is and could influence what it could be. It doesn't have to be the way it is.

But to explore concepts of Higher Consciousness may require the courage to go against the 'mindless' majority.

'No problem can be solved from the same consciousness that created it'.

Albert Einstein.

MENTAL DEFENCES

From an early age we find ourselves in the arena of life under threat. We either assimilate the experience and grow, with the appropriate response to pleasure or pain. Or we shy away and defend ourselves, resorting to psychological mechanisms which help us to throw some sort of protective shell round our fragile egos.

Such as withdrawal, hoping the problem (or challenge) will go away. Or rationalisation, using lame excuses to justify behaviour we are not proud of. Or projection, criticising our faults in others to deflect the flak. Or at the extreme, we may develop full-blown denial or nervous 'breakdown' to cope with what feels like unbearable trauma.

These 'mental devices for coping with stress' are understandable, even forgiveable. But they are not really helpful and they are not healthy. Only by 'getting real' can we recover our self-respect and equilibrium. Only by facing up to our fears and expressing them can we begin to grow. And it is not all pain; many of us are inhibited in our expression of love and joy.

We need to find the key to being spontaneous and natural as we once were. Then relationships will be more honest, open and fulfilling.

As the philosophies of Barry Long, Anthony de Mello and others maintain, we need to step out of the shadow of our fears and illusions into the sunshine of awareness, truth and joy.

And come Alive.

'Turn on the light of awareness and the darkness will disappear. Happiness is not something you acquire; love is not something you produce; love is not something you have. Love is something which has you. You do not have the wind, the stars, the rain. And surrender occurs when you are aware of your illusions, aware of your addictions, aware of your desires and fears'.

Anthony de Mello, 'Awareness'.

IDENTITY

Like any other powerful concept, Identity can have negative and positive aspects. At its worse and uncontrolled, it can lead to personal and national abuse of power with terrible consequences, as with excessive nationalism.

Yet if it is weak or absent in the individual, it will at best lead to a restless search to find it. At worse, its lack could precipitate mental illness.

Whether we find it through family ties, love, personal achievement or holistic therapies, its realisation defines us and gives others a guide as to how to respond to us. It is about feeling comfortable with our emotional and spiritual selves.

Based on a sense of intrinsic worth which has nothing to do with egotism.

Valuing ourselves. Feeling real.

Having identity.

Many 'alternative' approaches address this question, offering help when we finally ask the question 'Who am I?'

The answer has more to do with the higher self than with the facade of personality. It is the first step to coming alive.

'To know who one is, an individual must be aware of what they feel'.

Alexander Lowen.

THE NEED (2)

Most human beings need help; most human beings need to learn and grow, emotionally and spiritually. Most of us need to wake up and realise it.

A few advanced souls have already achieved this wisdom. But for most of us, Life - here and now - is the only arena where this can happen. It is a theatre of possibilities, the stage for our development towards enlightenment

Life is therefore in a sense a school, where all experience exists to enable us to achieve a state of light and grace. The challenge is to discern it in dark times.

If these concepts are considered together with the possibility - many would say probability - of progress through more than one life, plus the idea that what we sew we reap, then there can be a logic linking all.

But only if we are able and willing to penetrate the illusion and see.

'Spirituality. Waking up. And as I told you, it is extremely important, if you want to wake up, to go in for self-observation. Be aware of what you're saying, be aware of what you're doing, be aware of what you're thinking. Be aware of how you're acting. Be aware of where you're coming from, what your motives are. The unaware life is not worth living'.

Anthony de Mello, 'Awareness'.

SOUL PSYCHOLOGY

The latter half of the 20th C. has seen the realisation of a psychology of the soul.

Although the physical world deteriorates, the soul aspires to learn, develop and grow, always seeking to improve, as Maslow and others point out. Usually this is in material terms and therefore will always fall short of the dream.

Soul psychology embraces such concepts as self-actualisation (A. Maslow), higher and lower selves (R.Assiogli), child/adult/parent ego states (E. Berne), plus the power of healthy humility, which translates as a willingness to face up to whatever state of mind we are in (F. Perls). Help is useless unless we really want it and can see the need. In the religious sense, confession, repentance and forgiveness have always been powerful psychology.

Berne also talks about 'put-downs' and positive and negative strokes. This links with James Redfield's assertion that we need to feed on spiritual energy, derived both from each other and from higher sources.

The Higher Self, the indestructible plane of our nature, possesses wisdom, peace and joy. For most of humanity, the Lower Self strives to compete in this world, blind to these qualities and the existence of its other aspect.

During maturation, we develop the ego-states of child, adult and parent. The child is our initial state of ignorance and joy, also an innocent wisdom. Often our development is arrested at the stage of the hurt child, the cynical adult or the dogmatic, authoritarian parent. Many branches of religion and psychology say that we need to recover child-like qualities e.g. 'except you become as a little child you can not enter the Kingdom of Heaven' (Jesus). The Buddhist goal also is 'Beginners Mind'.

When we reach a point where we realise our existence is empty, that we need inspiration and that we can not do it alone, then the ground becomes fertile for the Divine seed to flourish. The outcome can be a reconciliation of higher and lower selves through insight and awareness.

Underlying all, of course, is the power and mystery of love.

'We can meditate and pray until we are old and grey - but without our Basic Self, we can never find the wholeness we are seeking. Spirituality can never be separated from psychology. Unless we deal with our emotional blockages, our childhood patterns, our negative and limiting beliefs, our spiritual growth will always be limited.'

from 'Stepping into the Magic'

AWARENESS

There are many levels of awareness and states of being: often referred to as 'altered (or alternative) states of consciousness'.

On the everyday level, the rational, 'thinking' mode is necessary for formal learning, earning a living and other practicalities. The trouble is, because of our anxieties, this kind of thinking becomes chronic, unless we realise it and seek the means to calm it.

Many people have found that when you seek the means to lay this chatterbox to rest at appropriate times, amazing things can happen.

In fact, with our eyes we look at life through a very narrow window, for visible light is only a fraction of the whole electro-magnetic spectrum.

There are many other planes beyond everyday awareness, some of which may be beneficially accessed. In the process, we are likely to discover aspects of ourselves of which we were unaware, so that we become fuller and wiser people. In other words, we may grow and realise more of our potential.

We need to balance the everyday world of activity and 'doing'; we must seek the stillness beyond thought.

And discover that stillness is not emptyness.

'With an eye made quiet by the power of harmony and the deep power of joy, we see into the life of things'.

W. Wordsworth

ALTERNATIVE STATES OF AWARENESS

There are many states of awareness other than that required for everyday living (and even that divides into applied thought and the free association of chatterbox communication).

From plain relaxation to deep mysticism, also the mood altering power of music and exercise, all of them cause alteration of the brain-wave patterns to greater or lesser degree.

Some of them may teach us much about ourselves and life, with the appropriate teacher, including

Day dreaming/Reverie
Recollection/Reminiscence
The just-before-sleep state
Sleep and dreams
Relaxation via various means
Visualisation/guided imagery
Meditation
Trance states
Movement (Exercise, dance)
Catharsis
Exhilaration and joy
'Beginner's mind'
Mystical experience
Enlightenment

'There are always at least two ways in'.

Co-counselling Course Leader.

HANDLING EMOTION

Although few realise it, the vast majority of us have a desperate need: to recognise and manage our emotional selves.

Our emotional make-up is the aspect of our nature which we understand least and which gives us most grief.

We think we are fulfilled by romantic or erotic love, then wonder why so many relationships founder. A relationship in which either party lacks understanding of their emotions hasn't much chance. In addition, we often unconsciously choose partners who supply the strength we lack. When they tire of doing so, or when we no longer have that weakness, the relationship may end.

There may be pain, but we are likely to be wiser and stronger as a consequence, for we become more complete and able to grow and move on.

Thus on an individual level, personal emotional understanding and development is crucial, leading to maturity, wisdom, peace and spiritual fulfillment.

It follows that human relationships at all levels and on a global scale would be less fraught, less prone to misunderstanding and disaster.

Seek the means.

'When we stop using our wills to push our strong emotions into unconsciousness, power and energy will be released and creative action will fill the space that was once occupied by tightness and tension'.

The Acorn Books

GROWTH, DEVELOPMENT AND PROGRESS

If human beings are largely asleep, or unaware of their essential nature; and their great needs are self-knowledge, emotional expression and personal development; then the alternatives are stagnation (which leads to deterioration) or progress.

There is an intimate relationship between self-awareness, personal development and emotional/spiritual growth: another of the triangles of life.

The 'Catch 22' is that there are really only two ways of coming alive and starting to become a fully-realised human being.

Either our complacency is fractured when we hit rock bottom, perhaps by a personal catastrophe which stops us in our tracks, bringing us face to face with our self and our need (and just pray there's someone around who can point the way to lasting solutions).

Or we open our hearts and minds a little to alternative life-styles and sample the goods. For only when we take a few faltering steps on the road to self-discovery can we begin to know the possibilities.

The choice is always yours.

'Experiencing feelings of rage and anger does not mean we must act them out. If we fully permit ourselves to experience the feelings as they arise, we ensure that our behaviour will be in proportion to the cause and appropriate to the situation.

The secret is making space and acceptance for all feelings to find wholeness.

Having acceptance means allowing .... emotions within our unconscious to reconnect with us; then they will be able to grow into understanding and wholeness through time'.

The Acorn Books.

TIME

In the early years, the mind of a child is timeless, which is both a blessing and a curse. There is forever to lose yourself in your activities; the only deadlines are imposed by adults. On the other hand, will something unpleasant ever end and how long do we have to wait to satisfy an immediate desire.

Time for adults is mostly a curse, a constant adversary. If time hangs heavy we are bored. If time runs out we miss a train, an opportunity or the chance of lasting satisfaction.

It is a constant battle which takes its toll, a constant striving to do, achieve, gain, keep ahead.

The alternative or complementary state is to Be. Certainly you can lose yourself briefly in activity or pleasure but eventually the Doing must cease and we are left with who and what we are. Inside the hurricane, there is total stillness. At the core of our in-most selves, there is truth and peace. To find and realise this by using healthy devices to drop out of time and the rat-race can enable us to develop our selves and our souls, even if this means adjusting our priorities and modifying the hurly-burly of living.

Eternal life is not so much concerned with everlasting time but with a continual state of being. The quality of our normal sensation, perception, living and being can be immeasurably enhanced, if we so desire.

'Eternal life means timeless - no time. The human mind can understand time and can deny time. What is timeless is beyond comprehension. Yet the mystics tell us that eternity is right now. How's that for good news? People are distressed when I tell them to forget their past; they are so proud of it. Or ashamed. that's crazy! When you hear 'Repent for your past!', it's a religious distraction from waking up. Wake up! That's what repent means. Not 'weep for your sins'. Wake up! Understand, stop all the crying. Understand! Wake up!'

Anthony de Mello, 'Awareness'.

ETERNAL LIFE

There is existence and there is Life: enthusiasm, spontaneity, vibrance, joy. The difference lies in degree of life quality and values.

The correct translation of Eternal is quality or depth of life, not only everlasting duration but the eternal Now. Can you do anything to enhance the quality of your Now?

We are meant to be fully alive, moment by moment, but many of us live in trance.

There are many ways of 'seeing the Light', being 'born again', achieving 'enlightenment' or 'having the scales fall from your eyes'. Doing so means moving from trance to reality, from existence to Life.

We need to seek the means to enhanced quality of life, to live at least part of the time on higher levels of consciousness.

Dreamer awake.

'I have come so that you might have Life and have it more abundantly'.

Jesus, The New Testament.

DILEMMA

The Human dilemma is that we are animals who often feel that we are much more than animals.

We must not discount the animals; they enrich our lives. Observing them and having their company can undoubtedly supply some of our spiritual need.

According to James Redfield, animals feed on energy physically, as in the natural world. Humans have a need for physical and psychological energy, often at others' expense. But what we really need is spiritual Energy from a higher source

We live in a physical, material world where competition and some exploitation seem necessary to survive. It contains at least as much deterioration and decay as creativity. And none of us get out of it alive. So what does anything matter.

Yet living this way does not seem to fulfil us. Only the realisation that part of us will always belong to a level above and beyond can help us make sense of it all. Living for the material eventually causes us to lose our self-respect deep down and a human being without self respect is either ineffective or dangerous.

Only the conviction that this life is necessary but temporary and that the indestructible part of us belongs to the spiritual realm can give us hope and peace.

One day, echoing Peter Marshall, we will exclaim with relief, gratitude, reverence and wonder, 'So it was true, it was You, all the time'

'Don't you see, we are worms whose insignificance lives but to form the angelic butterfly which flits to judgement naked of defence'.

Dante.

EVIDENCE AND CERTAINTY (1)

Regression techniques can enable people to become aware how past lives have affected the present and to realise how we were meant to learn and grow in this one.

The many recorded near-death experiences can illuminate our darkness and ignorance. Most who have these visions return inspired, feeling it is for a purpose.

Mystical moments are experienced not only by the religious but by scientists and many ordinary people, who have managed to create the necessary conditions of reverence/humility, gentle self discipline, a positive outlook and an attitude of discreet service.

Intuition and inspiration are direct channels from Spirit.

Imagination and creativity, used with humility, are not only inspired by the Spirit, they are the stuff of Life.

Many Spiritual teachers have taught through allegory - God's hidden messages, indicating wonderful things to those that have eyes to see. And in nature there are great metaphors; the sun always shines beyond the clouds.

Synchronicity is direct but subtle guidance via miracles and magic, perhaps mirroring the sub-atomic level. Divination may operate this way too.

Humour springing from Joy is a spiritual characteristic and unique to human beings.

Finally, many of us who have been privileged to enable people to be what they are capable of, have been humbled by the intrinsic worth of humanity and its potential.

'We move on the fringes of eternity and we are sometimes granted vistas through the fabric of illusion'.

from Cathedrals of the Spirit, by Teri Mcluhan.

EVIDENCE AND CERTAINTY (2)

We may not always like the way life operates, but generally intelligence and logic underlie creation on this level. In general, well ordered patterns underpin our existence. It is illogical that life, brought into existence with such effort and with such a blue-print, is without a higher purpose, therefore a pre-life and an after-life are possibilities.

Furthermore, cause and effect is a universal logic that affects many levels and spheres of life, from the microcosm to the macrocosm, physically, psychologically and spiritually.

Another absolute is that nothing can ever be destroyed, merely changed to a different form.

Life deteriorates physically in order to be born again but, from a Spiritual aspect, it always seeks to improve, grow, develop, progress and transcend. This may involve dying more than once in one way or another.

If the evidence for a much wider spiritual backdrop to this life is 50-50, then these factors at least tip the balance to 51-49. In such a Yes - No situation, this may as well be 99 - 1, making the possible the probable.

So what is there to lose?

'God does not die on the day we cease to believe in a personal deity. But we die on the day our lives cease to be illuminated by the steady radiance of wonder renewed daily, the source of which is beyond all reason'.

Dag Hammerskold.

RE-INCARNATION

One life doesn't make sense, certainly not if there is point and purpose to it all.

If there is a point to life, it is about learning, growing, developing and progressing. Yet life's deck of cards favours some more than others; the playing field is not even. So more than one life is essential, not only for fairness and justice, but to ensure that we are all exposed to the experience necessary for our stage of development. For what we sow, we reap; that is Karma.

One chance, take it or leave it, is illogical. As is a belief that life is purely physical or material. Not only does it pall and fail to really satisfy as such, but it goes no-where. There is no end or goal. 'Eat, drink and be merry for tomorrow we die' is rubbish. What does such an attitude gain if we are snuffed out? Not that life should not be enjoyed, for doing so can be a form of worship and we can learn much spiritually by fully utilising our senses. But it should not become an end in itself, or the object is defeated.

The hedonistic philosophy has no gain - particularly if we have a short memory! - apart from blotting out reality and damaging body, mind and spirit. There may also be regret, as we take our last breath that we took all and gave nothing back. In the dying words of Elizabeth I of England, 'All my possessions for a moment of time'. Or to paraphrase the words of Jesus, 'How do you benefit if you gain the world and lose your soul?'

Reincarnation also solves the problem of survival, though not necessarily of our little ego and personality.

'Individuality itself seemed to dissolve and fade away into boundless being : this was not a confused state but the clearest of the clear, the surest of the sure, utterly beyond words - where death was almost a laughable impossibility - the loss of personality (if so it were) seeming no extinction but the only true life'.

Alfred Lord Tennyson

HELPING

On the face of it, being kind to someone else seems like a good idea. Life is hard and we could all do with a little help.

But are help and kindness one and the same thing ?

At one end of the scale, too much help can be interference, taking over and eroding the chances of the other to gain the lasting benefit and satisfaction of helping themselves.

With children, this can damage their long-term chances of confidence and independence. Suffocating, interfering help can increase helplessness, causing frustration and resentment. It is often delivered so that the helper can feel and be seen to be good. It is much harder to stand by and give practical assistance minimally and discreetly.

At the other extreme, there is Altruism; apparently unselfish help, concern, love. Even such noble acts may be performed because we simply could not stand living with the alternative, as when rescuing someone from a fire. We are selfish in the sense that we put ourselves in their place. Or even if we perish, we have placed someone for ever in our debt. Even the love of parent for child may be because they are our flesh and we have invested so much time and effort in them. We see them as an extension of our own personality and ego.

We are likely to have a frustrated life in the end if we always do things for an eventual pay-off in Heaven. Even this is selfish. Only if we act because we believe that life isn't worth living without practical goodness, because we feel it is up to us to set an example, because someone has to do it, or because Service is a basic Law of the Universe, is there any merit.

Failing this, it is at least honest to admit some benefit to us in the act of helping. Then both parties will be happier and feel less guilty.

'Selfishness is not living as one wishes to live. It is asking others to live as one wishes to live. And unselfishness is letting other people's lives alone, not interfering with them'.

Oscar Wilde

LOVING AND GIVING

"Love thy neighbour as thyself" has long been mis-interpreted.

It does not necessarily mean Love thy Neighbour more than thyself, although many must have thought this was a quick way to heaven and led a most frustrating and unfulfilled life. The only justification for this might be if this world was of no consequence.

Jesus also taught that we had to make the most of this world and the talents we were born with. We can never do this by neglecting or ill-treating ourselves.

It is our duty to actively realise our possibilities, our potential, and rejoice in our selfness. Although we should not intentionally hurt others, we should seek first to find the Kingdom of God within us. We should respect ourselves, be kind to ourselves and love ourselves, without egotism. If we don't, we may be bitter and unfulfilled. How then can we love anyone and how can we expect anyone to love us? We must love the potential for Good in ourselves.

Many try to give when their resources are depleted. We must ensure we have enough in the bank, physically, mentally and spiritually. Only when our own cup runs over will we have more than enough of sufficient quality to share with others. The means exist.

'Ask and you shall receive. Seek and you shall find. Knock and it shall be opened to you'

Jesus, The New Testament.

MUSIC

Music is the mediator between the spiritual and the sensual life.

Beethoven

All one's life is music if one touches the notes rightly and in tune

J Ruskin

Music is the one incorporeal entrance into
the higher world of knowledge which
comprehends mankind but which mankind
can not comprehend.

Beethoven.

Music alone with sudden charms can bind
The wandering sense, and calm
the troubled mind.

Hymn to Harmony

There is sweet music here that softer falls
Than petals from blown roses on the grass,
Or night-dew on still waters between walls
Of shadowy granite, in a gleaming pass;
Music that gentler on the spirit lies
Than tired eyelids upon tired eyes.

Alfred Lord Tennyson.

A FRIEND......

......is one who knows you as you are

understands where you've been,

accepts who you've become

....and still gently invites you to grow.

Anonymous.

A friend is one who knows you as you are, but likes you anyway.

Anonymous

BEREAVEMENT

Loss of someone near can mean despair, anger, emptiness, depression, hopelessness. Even a physical pain, the gnawing hunger of loss.

Strange how impoverished we are in dealing with such strong emotions, for apparently intelligent beings with supposedly high-level communication.

Special words can and do help in some cases, but we are all different. The need is beyond mere intellect: it is a spiritual problem and needs spiritual answers. It needs the direct, intuitive communication of feeling between soul and soul.

The only other means we have are touch and eyes and intuition: the transfer of warmth and energy, the reassurance of just being there. By the giving of time and self. By silent support and shared pain.

'Surrounded as you are by helpers from every kingdom and from many dimensions, you still insist on walking alone, eyes downcast, in self-imposed exile.

Look up, look inward and your exile and loneliness will be at an end'.

The Acorn Books.

WORDS AND SOUND

Words are symbols for concepts and feelings. That means they are only second-hand attempts to represent actual experience; approximations to Reality and Truth.

Great literature and poetry may at times inspire but, in everyday life, words are often crude, damaging and misinterpreted, giving rise to disastrous misunderstandings. Communication, on the surface glib and easy, is in fact complex and difficult. Yet words are our principle means of expression.

But words also carry great power. The power of Thought, for thought is energy; and the power of Sound.

The energy of sound has pervaded life and nature from the Creation - 'In the beginning was the Word' - and human beings have been given a measure of this power and its manipulation. Through our voices we have the subtle ability to modulate sound to induce powerful effects in ourselves and others, especially so in tandem with instruments. Whether it be for military purposes, a Handel Oratorio, the gut stimulus of electronic rock, the chanting of a Buddhist mantra, or a variety of alternative approaches and therapies which use sound and voice to heal and help, we should not underestimate the power and privilege of these gifts.

'The most grossly neglected energy source on earth is human energy. You possess greater powers than you imagine. Thought for instance; your thoughts can heal or cripple, nourish or destroy. Wield them wisely, always remembering that the twin of power is responsibility'.

The Acorn Books.

POWER AND CONTROL

How bitterly ironic that man can now finely control great natural forces, yet can hardly regulate his own nature or that of his race.

We can control nuclear fission but not the world population. We have the means but not the will.

We can stop a vehicle in yards from 100 MPH, but not prevent the mayhem in a casualty department on a Saturday night.

We can cross an ocean at the speed of sound but not respect or be civil to each other.

We can reach the moon but only cause hell on earth.

We can create the tension of bottled up emotion but not seek the means to safely and productively deal with it.

We can see many things but not always the Truth.

Until the Controller is subject to self-regulation, the outlook is bleak.

The means exist.

'He who, dwelling in all things,
Yet is other than all things:
Whom all things do not know,
Whose body all things are,
Who controls all things from within -
He is your Soul, the Inner Controller.
The Immortal'.

Brihad-anranyaka Upanishad.

LIVING LIGHTLY

Fact 1: Everything has positive and negative aspects.

Fact 2: Anything carried to excess can at the least become harmful, at worst a vice or a monster e.g.

Food can nourish or cause obesity and illness.

Science can be beneficial or cause havoc.

Organisation can raise the level of our civilisation but institutionalisation can seriously damage people.

Love can bring out our potential or cloy and suffocate.

All of these are aspects of power or energy and there is a relationship between power, privilege and responsibility, another of life's triangles.

The privilege of power must be used with foresight, insight and humility. We must know that such gifts, if used irresponsibly, will destroy. Weilding them wisely and in balance can be a factor in our spiritual growth.

We should never grasp and try to possess them, but appreciate and utilise them with joy and gratitude.

'He who binds to himself a joy
Does the winged life destroy.
He who kisses the joy as it flies
Lives in Eternity's sunrise'.

William Blake.

RESPONSIBILITY

Some fight shy of it. Others thrive on it. Somebody has to take it.

Given in graduated doses, it can be the making of a youngster; enabling them to explore the boundaries of their personality, come to terms with their limitations and develop their talents and strengths.

In fact, self-knowledge, personal development and spiritual growth are all linked to assuming responsibility - responsibility for ourselves, our emotions and our relationships.

To do so we need to explore ourselves, our feelings and attitudes. This can be a bumpy ride, for which we may need to seek a guide or support group. But it can be a liberating journey, to the light at the end of the tunnel. It can spell freedom - from prejudice, guilt, fear and dependence.

If we make the commitment, we may find we have gained response-ability: the ability to respond openly, honestly and spontaneously to life.

Joy, sensitivity and creativity are the fruits.

'I was angry with my friend;
I told my wrath, my wrath did end.
I was angry with my foe;
I told it not; my wrath did grow'.

William Blake

BEING HUMAN

I would like the world to be full of harmony and happiness. I would like people to be fulfilled and content. I honestly would; sounds naive perhaps but, if many children had their way, that is how it would be.

But I have so much self-centredness (not the same as deliberate selfishness) because of fears and insecurities that I seem to make little effective contribution to making this Global vision possible. What I try to do seems to blow away in the wind.

Romantic love is often narrow, shutting the world out. At its best it can provide a secure base from which to reach out to the world. It can also reduce the bitterness of unfulfilment; unfortunately it can go wrong and work the other way.

Pre-requisites to the ability to love widely include early security, space, guidance and encouragement of healthy discipline, freedom, support, opportunity and democracy. There are two further elements necessary for a Human Being to be fully who they are: Attention and Non-judgement.

Attention means listening and noticing (and allowing time to do so), with humility and genuineness. It means allowing a person to be who they truly are. Total attention creates an atmosphere which allows and encourages a person to be and express themselves fully. Carl Rogers described this as 'unconditional positive regard'.

Non-judgement implies acceptance, with no pre-conceived ideas, which means allowing and giving permission for feeling and communication i.e. being fully Human: something which many of us, in our closed-down state, may never have experienced.

A child reared on these terms is less likely to grow into a demanding adult. When unconditional attention and acceptance are present, so much promise and potential may be realised.

'Love is a way of being
And more than that It is simply being,
Being with another person, however they may be
Holding no hidden agendas
No need to have them experience your love
No desire to demonstrate love
No intrusion upon their soul
Nothing but acceptance of their being
Born of your acceptance of yours.'

The Acorn Books

ACCEPTANCE

It is not easy to set our prejudices aside and accept another completely, to allow them to find themselves. It is no easier for them to show their true selves, but to do so is many times easier if Love can be unconditional, for trust then has a chance.

Only in that atmosphere can a person grow, blossom and reach their potential. There is so much Human potential being stunted. There is much truth in the saying 'Criticism is like a sharp frost on a child's spirit' (although perhaps this should be qualified as negative or insensitive criticism). We are all children at heart; the danger is developing people with shells so hard that they can never be reached.

It may be difficult to show this kind of love to some adults who appear to have been damaged beyond repair yet love, in the form of calculated trust, has been known to induce spectacular changes in people.

But the child has a right to love with few strings; the future depends on it.

'If you love it, let it go.
If it returns, it was yours;
If it doesn't, it never was'.

Anonymous.

LOVE AT ALL COSTS?

So is Unconditional Love the answer to everything? And does that mean that anyone be permitted to get away with anything?

The problem is that this world is less than perfect: thus measures, often severe, may have to be taken to increase the chances of someone taking a close look at themselves, perhaps for the first time.

When we do look inward to see what and where we are and what we could be, in the right milieu and with the right teacher, the result is likely to be change for the better.

Often the transformation is spectacular.

What society is largely ignorant of are the means to combine or replace purely penal measures with effective, self-motivated, spiritually-based behavioural change.

Even now, a few brave pioneers are using the proven powerful emotional and spiritual techniques of the new psychology, bringing together both perpetrators and victims of crimes, to attempt some sort of reconciliation and healing. Much may be learned by all parties in the process and it is Love that triumphs.

'If you bring forth what is within you, it will save you. What you do not bring forth will destroy you'.

from The Gospel of Thomas.

HATE

Hate is a combination of fear and anger. You can have fear without hate and anger without hate, but both together develop a new and dangerous dimension.

For hate is of course the antithesis of love. Indeed shallow and superficial or merely erotic love can soon turn into hate.

But love without conditions, that does not count the cost, bears no malice. It arises from, and gives rise to, true security.

Where there is security, fear and anger vanish; just as early mist has no chance before the warm sun of a summer morning.

'The day will come when, after harnessing the winds, the tides and gravitation, we shall harness for God the energies of Love. On that day, for the second time in the history of the world, man will have discovered fire'.

Teilhard de Jardin.

CONFLICT

To resolve this chronic condition or affliction of humanity needs a rare soul with more experience and erudition than most of us. In the main, it is damaging, divisive and destructive.

Yet there can be positive aspects. Improved attitudes, relationships and respect, even renewal of love, can be a consequence, especially when guided by someone who knows about these things.

Perhaps the existence of conflict is even designed to teach us something about both ourselves and our antagonist, affording a valuable learning opportunity.

We can reflect on several relevant maxims:

'Them that have eyes to see, let them see'. Just as a thunderstorm can clear the air, so conflict can be a factor in clearing our vision, causing us to alter our illusions, delusions and prejudices and put in perspective the faults not only of our opponent but ourselves.

'No conflict can be resolved from the same consciousness in which it started'. There must be understanding, compromise and giving (forgiveness). A win-win situation needs to be created, so that no-one feels put down.

'To change everything, simply change your attitude'. Incredibly simple, incredibly hard. In the process of reconciliation, ' the two become one'.

'Conflict exists only to increase consciousness'.

C. G. Jung.

FORGIVENESS

is the hardest thing in the world. The same as loving unconditionally.

If my brother was blown up or my child killed in a hit and run, I would feel murderous. I would feel the need for revenge and justice. But revenge is of the gut, justice of the mind. We may also feel that there is little you can do for the victim but you can at least try to ensure it never happens again.

You don't only do that by putting away the perpetrator for life. Often they are themselves victims of circumstances so, if we can understand the causes, not only will the question 'Why' be answered but there is a chance of redress, learning and future prevention if not cure. That is preferable to mere justice.

Revenge and violence breed revenge and violence. It is a vicious circle, only stopped when reason and spirituality come into play. Jesus said we should forgive 'seventy times seven'. In the long run, forgiveness, tolerance and love breed forgiveness, tolerance and love.

It is like fighting a forest fire or an insidious disease: a gap has to be created in the chain of transmission.

'Forgiveness is another word for letting go. We are saved by forgiveness, the power to forgive ourselves, to allow ourselves to be forgiven, which matures into the power to forgive others and allow them their time to be forgiven. Forgiveness is about letting go of fear. There is no healing, no salvation, without forgiveness. And with forgiveness, all things become saved and healed once again.'

Mathew Fox.

JUDGEMENT

The concepts of judgement and justice in our lives and in the Universe are both more complex and more simple than our dogmatic, vengeful perspective allows, borne of insecurity and a narrow, self-centred viewpoint of fairness.

For whatever reasons, we have difficulty in seeing the greater Whole, perhaps mercifully. The pressures of life make it difficult to be objective and see all standpoints. Only between lives and in the context of reincarnation is this possible.

Between lives, Love prevails. Even our 'Judgement', takes place in an atmosphere of pure love. Furthermore it is mainly we who judge ourselves, with a little help from our Higher friends, who enable us to see much further than we can here.

Certainly, we may be tortured by what we see, but only good can come of it. For we will be enabled to plan our spiritual futures, perhaps returning to restore the balance or to serve by enabling someone else to achieve insight and enlightenment.

'All things work together for good to them that love God'.

The New Testament.

GRACE

Grace, like Love, is one of those fascinating concepts which are easier to recognise or sense than describe or define. They almost elude words and can only be inferred or hinted at.

Grace, like light, pervades every corner of life, indeed may be the difference between life and mere existence. It is present when we recognise, consciously or otherwise, that certain elements blend perfectly, that something couldn't be more right, that the Whole is infinitely more than the sum of of its parts. When something is elegantly simple and inspired. When we know we are in the presence of unsurpassed quality.

Grace is Love that comes out of the blue. That continues in spite of everything. Grace is help that comes from an unexpected source or at an unexpected time.

It may be manifest in the purely physical as in the un-selfconsciousness of a child, the charm of femininity or the consummate movement of a supreme athlete.

Grace infers perfection, symmetry and mastery, seemingly without effort. The ideal, whether of form or being or behaviour. But it could also describe the generosity of Spirit of someone as deformed as The Elephant Man.

It implies mercy and unselfish love, as when someone with every benefit genuinely reaches those with few; the King who kissed the leper.

'One Nature, perfect and pervading, circulates in all natures, one Reality, all-comprehensive, contains within itself all realities. The one Moon reflects itself wherever there is a sheet of water, And all the moons in the waters are embraced within the one Moon. The Inner Light is beyond praise and blame: Like space, it knows no boundaries,

Yet it is even here within us, ever retaining its serenity and fullness. It is only when you hunt for it you that you lose it; You cannot take hold of it, but equally you cannot get rid of it'.

Yung-chia Ta-shih.

QUALITY

The world is imperfect, but wherever Spirit touches it, quality shows through.

There is existence and there is life. Quality is the difference: when quality is reduced, life is diminished.

It is love (of life, self and others) gives rise to concern and care, and care results in quality. Love, Care and Quality are linked in a triangular relationship; triangles are the most secure geometry.

A pseudo-quality, usually related to material goods, can be imitated by devising ever tighter systems, allied to fear (e.g. of job loss). But it is quality without soul and to the detriment of those involved, because their hearts are not in it.

Love often gives rise to inspiration and quality is often inspired by love.

Thank God for Quality. It enhances and enriches life, giving it the quality of spirituality. It nourishes our souls.

'Pride makes us do things well. But it is love which makes us do things to perfection'

H. Jackson Brown.

INSPIRATION

Inspiration resembles Spiritual oxygen. In fact, the word is closely akin to the concept of breathing, for inspiration + expiration = respiration. Our spirit can be seen as the receiver and transmitter of inspiration; under the right conditions, inspiration flows through Spirit to the rest of our being.

When oxygen reaches the cells, in effect it lights them up, as it does with any fire. The spirit needs inspiration, so that our world may be illuminated, on a personal and a global level. More specifically, Spirit needs to be allowed to infuse the other levels of our being; thus lighting up - and lightening - our personality.

The root 'spir' is also found in 'spirit' and 'aspire'. It implies, at the risk of being twee, 'a desire to aspire to the higher'; to lift ourselves, to connect to the higher and the finer, rather than the base, the gross and the coarse. We can however learn valuable lessons through the tribulations of our lower self.

It is also synonymous with creativity, i.e. to generate and to give life to, to produce, to construct. Most writers and artists, even some scientists, tell us they don't know where their ideas come from. It's as if they have the ability to tap into a vein of inspiration on another level.

Implicit in inspiration are the twin concepts of life and joy. 'He or she was inspired' means they are living as if their feet don't touch the ground. If that sounds as if they are not realistic, it is inspiration that helps them meet the challenges and the grief of life and cope with the mundane.

'The Kingdom (of Heaven) is a state of transformed consciousness'.

Jesus, The Gnostic Gospels.

THE FEMININE

Although they are complementary, it is a fact that in most societies the feminine has been subservient to the masculine for centuries. The formal, the authoritarian and the paternal have long held sway at the expense of sensitivity and insight.

At either extreme and without the influence of the other, both are lost and dangerous. In tandem, they approach the nature of the Divine, steering the middle way of love, through which all things are possible.

We have seen what masculine energy and power can do without feminine moderation. The pendulum is swinging: let us pray it will find its harmonious mid-point.

For humanity badly needs the civilising quality of feminine wisdom, the spiritualising influence of feminine insight.

Therein lies Wholeness; unity depends on it.

'A fully realised human being is one who, in the words of Lao Tzu, 'knows the masculine and yet keeps to the feminine'.

Fritzof Capra, 'The Tao of Physics'.

THE BODY

It is a cliche to say that the body is the temple of the soul. It is many things. A space suit and life-support system. An envelope for feelings, emotions, mind, spirit. A reservoir and record of the emotional and physiological effects of every life-event. Armour plating.

If these feelings and effects are not discharged, they can become chronic. Our muscles and tissues literally become locked and rigid, giving varying degrees of pain and immobility which may manifest and masquerade as tension, rheumatics and 'mystery ailments'.

This dis-ease is also reflected in other areas of life. Perhaps in our whole attitude.

Often, with the right teacher or therapist, the dis-ease can be undone. Sometimes the approach is physical, sometimes emotional or spiritual, sometimes all three.

The result can be the same: the freeing of tissues, emotions. And the Spirit.

'If you are an alive body, no-one can tell you how to experience the world. And no-one can tell you what truth is, because you experience it for yourself.

The body does not lie'.

Stanley Keleman.

TOUCH

Human life depends on contact for its perpetuation and its emotional quality. Touch in fact literally enlivens us and enriches our lives, together with its corollary, verbal communication.

Pre - birth, we are cosseted for 9 months, protected, nourished: all our needs supplied. Then we are separated, fairly traumatically, from this warm, safe contact, this Love.

Cast out into a relatively alien environment, where the contact we crave is at a distance and at a premium. Granted in most cases mother-love is still available for a time at least and we soon learn with the few weapons we have in our helplessness to manipulate and perhaps abuse it. But generally contact now has to be worked for and earned, by effort and within the rules.

After we learn to talk, speech will 'get us into contact' with people and, if we are good with words, we may persuade and woo and become intimate with others, although words can also create barriers and many misunderstandings.

But in the important years before speech, touch is primary and paramount. However old we are, there is always a child within us, which deserves much more recognition than it receives. There is no substitute for a cuddle or simply an arm round the shoulders in comfort. There is no substitute for physical contact and ultimately it may be the direct way, the only way, through the barriers.

Touch, and the many holistic therapies that derive from it, can be the direct route not only to reassuring comfort but to intense spiritual experience.

'Man has no body distinct from his soul'

William Blake.

WHOLE, HEALTHY, HAPPY.

Mind, body and spirit are not separate. They are inter-dependent and each expressed through - and often nourished by - the others.

Unfortunately life has the effect of fragmenting or disconnecting these aspects of self. This is not a healthy state and in fact can damage the immune system, thus initiating a vicious circle.

The recovery of integration, wholeness and health is theoretically simple.

First become aware that there is a need, that we are not fully in touch with our selves and our souls. Many people believe that to know ourselves thus is a reason, or pre-requisite, for our life on earth.

Then we must seek the help to rectify the unifying factor in our makeup - our feelings and emotions. Most human-beings carry long-standing, often deep-seated, emotional garbage that needs dealing with.

Doing so restores health, happiness and Wholeness, together with our connections with the Divine and the Universe, for it too operates as a unified Whole.

'The unaware life is not worth living'

Socrates.

HEALTH, HEALING, WHOLENESS

Before Betty Shine, the renowned spiritual healer, realised she was psychic, she suffered considerable ill-health. When she accepted the fact and gave in to the forces urging her to develop her gifts, her health immediately improved. Hers is not an isolated case.

There is much evidence that a lot of the ill-health in the world is due to being out of contact with the forces of harmony.

This is not to decry the role of conventional medicine, but if it worked more in tandem with alternatives, it might be needed less and human well-being would be enhanced. Holistic approaches at least nourish the Spirit, a need which is increased in ill-health.

Neither field is an exact science or a perfect art and there is much to learn. Miracles can and do happen but at present can not be guaranteed, perhaps because our insight is imperfect.

This will only improve when we open our hearts and minds in co-operation with each other and to higher energies.

'Greater things than these shall you do....'

Jesus, The New testament.

ADDICTION

What more can be said about habits that enslave. They are a tragedy and such a waste of life and potential.

If at an early age children can be shown the variety, wonder and fascination of life, if they can develop at least one talent, if they can be respected and listened to and if they can be encouraged to be either courageous or just plain awkward and individual in resisting peer pressure and following like sheep, then there is a chance. Schools, parents and governments may have to change, but so be it.

Perhaps we all need our fixes and crutches. The good news is that non-addictive 'highs' can be achieved without poisons or destructive means.

Using psycho-spiritual means, we can connect with higher sources of energy which uplift and inspire us. We can find ourselves living on a different plane, often surprisingly easily. It can be mind-blowing and once discovered does not readily go away.

Our lives, attitudes and relationships can be changed beyond recognition, bringing clarity, fulfillment and joy.

Strangely, this naturally altered state of perception does not cause us to be out of touch; it actually enhances our contact with reality and we are glad of it.

'Come home to yourself. Observe yourself......self-observation is such a delightful and extra-ordinary thing. After a while, you don't have to make any effort. Because, as illusions begin to crumble, you begin to know things that can not be described. It's called happiness. Everything changes and you become addicted to awareness'.

Anthony de Mello, 'Awareness'.

THROUGH THE KEYHOLE

The material world is hard reality - or is it?

When science takes it apart, all that is revealed is empty space and energy.

Wonderful as they are, all that we have to perceive this apparent reality are our sense organs: instruments which can directly perceive only a fraction of what is going on in our Universe.

The wavelengths on which our vision operates comprise only a fraction of the electro-magnetic spectrum. It is like looking at what is going on through a crack or keyhole. This means there are many phenomena 'beyond our ken'.

Of course we have contrived other means of information-gathering, yet science now finds that if ultimate Truth is ever to be known, it will not only be through taking things further and further apart, by greater analysis, but by taking an integrated and holistic view.

It is said we are 'ghosts in a machine'. If a ghost is something transitory and illusory, then human beings fit the bill. Here today, gone tomorrow, without trace in the sands of time.

Could it be that we are observers who belong to a more permanent state of being than this limited and elusive sphere?

Our birth is but a sleep and a forgetting
The soul that rises with us, our life's star
Hath had elsewhere it setting
And cometh from afar.

Not in entire forgetfulness,
And not in utter nakedness
Bur trailing clouds of glory do I come,
From God who is our home.

William Wordsworth.

MISCONCEPTIONS

Cleverness is not necessarily wisdom
Simple is not necessarily stupid
Fun is not necessarily happiness
Merriment is not necessarily joy
Laughter is not necessarily humour
Teasing is not necessarily amusing
Rest is not necessarily relaxation
Quietness is not necessarily boring
Seriousness is not necessarily morbid
Dogma is not necessarily truth
Wealth is not necessarily riches
Having it all is not necessarily contentment
... add your own.

'Not all that glistens ... is gold.

Thomas Gray

JUST AROUND THE CORNER

The path to a new vision of life, to heightened awareness, to a new consciousness, can be very short.

If conducive conditions are created, it may be almost instantaneous, or certainly within days. This however is usually in a group situation; the energy of the group seems to focus and accelerate the process.

If the influence for spiritual change is from a higher plane, it may also be that this plane is not far removed from our everyday level of living. It could even be adjacent and complementary to it, but on different wavelengths. A case of 'now you see the parallel universe, now you don't.

But the more we live joyously, the more wisdom we achieve, the more we are likely to see.

In this sense, 'the good life' could be literally 'just around the corner', as many have discovered.

'If the eye is unobstructed, the result is hearing. If the nose is unobstructed, the result is a sense of smell. If the mouth is unobstructed, the result is taste. If the mind is unobstructed, the result is wisdom'

Anthony de Mello, 'Awareness'.

COMPLEMENTARY, ALTERNATIVE, HOLISTIC

The 'alternative' scene provokes a varied response. Some find it boring, others disturbing. Yet it can mean hope and joy for many who have sampled its varied facets.

The Holistic spectrum is wide-ranging, from the physical, to the psychological, to the spiritual (holistic implies the interdependence of these aspects) and from the quiet and relaxing to the active and exhilarating.

Some approaches are ancient and mystical, others cutting-edge psychology; strangely these may overlap or dovetail, again emphasising holism. Many practitioners are eclectic, their intuition determining the methods, depending on individual need and response.

The Alternative field does appear to fill a human need, bordering on the spiritual; despite its imperfections it would not survive if it was not of benefit. At the very least it provides comfort. In some instances, there appear to be cures verging on the miraculous; perhaps research is needed to determine factors involved in increasing the consistency of such outcomes.

Most Complementary approaches do no harm, although caution needs to be exercised in therapies where emotions are exposed. Either a support network needs to be established or the practitioner needs to be not only ethical but committed.

No doubt there are charlatans and fast-buck merchants in the field. These can be weeded out by personal recommendation and of course if it doesn't start to work for you fairly soon, then cut your losses.

In the end there is no one way, only your way. All that matters is that it works for you. If it does, you are unlikely ever to be the same again.

'There are more things in Heaven and Earth.....than are dreamt of in your philosophy'.

Shakespeare, 'Hamlet'.

COUNSELLING

Although counselling is offered quite widely these days, it is not highly valued by the majority. The feeling seems to be   that humanity has survived war and tragedy since time began and that 'giving in' by accepting counselling is wimpish, if not weird.

It is of course a modern phenomenon, a product of the late 20th C. On the surface it is an off-shoot of psychotherapy (which also has a poor press), which assumes that people are sick and need an expert to cure them, the power being with the expert.

However it is also a consequence of increasing human sensitivity, a manifestation of our spiritual evolution. The race is slowly becoming more aware. It started with education. Then democracy. Then campaigning for rights, which has been the theme of the 20th C. The outcome is increased awareness of our selves, our emotions, our relationships and what makes them work.

Greater sensitivity makes the world a better place and this 'waking up' may be what it is all about. But it means we shut out and bottle up the effects of trauma and abuse at our peril. There is always a price to pay.

There are good and less good counsellors. But someone with the right personality, skills and motivation can help us to clarify issues, clear blockages and assist us in identifying and utilising our inner resources to move forward. Counsellors are not necessarily academic experts but guides who can empathise and facilitate through a grasp of the essence of communication, emotions and relationships.

Counselling is about empowerment, but the power and choice are always with the individual.

'The faith of the counsellors is love'.

The Faith of the Counsellors.

85

THE TAO

According to Lao Tsu in The Tao te Ching, 'Man follows earth. Earth follows heaven. Heaven follows the the Tao. The Tao follows what is natural'.

Everything, including ourselves, consists of energy. That energy manifests as pulses, waves, rythms, patterns. It has been called 'the dance of Life'.

Tao means The Way: the life lived in harmony with the laws of the Universe.

To achieve this harmony, we need to discern these patterns, rythms and laws and attune ourselves to them, for we are meant to be part of the dance. All we have to be is ourselves, as we were in the beginning.

That is the Way to fulfill our destiny.

'Re-attune yourselves to the pulse of the Universe. It beats within all vibrations: everything is pervaded by it - even yourselves. You have simply ceased to hear it, to feel it beating all round you. This heart-beat of the Universe pulses through all worlds seen and unseen, through galaxies within and without. All living creatures gladly respond to it - except man.

Why are you afraid, what have you to lose?'

The Acorn Books.

OPTIMISM

If you seek the confidence and serenity of ultimate certainty despite the evidence of our narrow, self-centred viewpoint, consider:

* Because intelligence exists, logically life must make ultimate sense, and sense implies order and harmony.

* Nothing can be destroyed, it only changes form. And all the pain, deterioration and change in the world eventually leads only to new life and re-creation.

* Despite the horrors of life, often caused by blind, ignorant, fearful humanity, joy and love keep re-emerging. It seems joy, love and life itself can never be extinguished. The sun always shines beyond the clouds.

* The revelations and transformations, afforded to those who seek, result in an intuitive certainty about human destiny which, once experienced, can never be taken away.

*'Remember always – not with my speech,
not with my eyes, not even with my mind
will that Self be reached. It will declare itself
to me only in my stillness'.*

Katha Upanishad.

NEW CONSCIOUSNESS

'The Old Order Changeth'. For all its faults, the old was more secure if only because change was slower. Strange how we need both change and challenge, but also security and stability.

Yet now there seems no control over change and it is not clear where we are heading. The old means of support, guidance and social control have been discredited and dismantled and the vehicle now seems to have faulty brakes and steering. If the vehicle is Spaceship Earth, it is also being increasingly abused. Perhaps we deserve to be cast adrift on an island in space for our sins.

Therefore we have to work it out. The future is up for grabs and it is getting late. All destruction can be an opportunity to re-create and all the materials are still available. There has been destruction before and much wisdom was lost, or at least went underground for those who were determined to find it.

'New Age' thought, attitudes, philosophy and relationships may help us recover and restore those Truths. But not the connotations that connect with seedy, hedonistic hippy hangovers from the 60s: New Age means wonder, truth, reality, spirituality, sensitivity and humanity. A New or Higher Consciousness.

In practice, recovery of age-old values.

'We were shown our destiny before we descended into earth embodiment. Thus we may assume that those who have associated themselves with the spiritual movement for the New Age must assuredly have had a preview of the stupendous events of the closing decades of the (20th) century and have consciously undertaken the task of living through this great period. Many respond to the New Age vision because, deep down in their soul they know the Truth. What a generation to be alive!'

Sir George Trevelyan.

KOANS AND THE MYSTERY OF LIFE

Buddhist philosophy uses 'koans' to cultivate enlightenment in its followers. Koans are insoluble problems e.g. What is the sound of one hand clapping? They are intended to show up the limitations of the logical mind. Usually, mirroring the way most of us use our minds in an obsessional way, the disciple fiercely tackles the challenge, often for a long time. The ego is unwilling to accept defeat.

At the point of utter frustration, if and when he gives up, he realises the pointlessness and stupidity of his efforts. He may also suddenly see in his ensuing mindlessness that there is a Universe of experience beyond the smallness of his mind. He also finds that the world still exists and life goes on despite all his efforts and his failure.

Such exercises put the mind in perspective, if not in its place. It is a valuable tool when used appropriately, a good servant but a bad master, unless we find out how to switch it off. Our world does not end when we do so.

The mystery of Life is a koan, which may be designed to do just this. For at that point of surrender, we connect with the wisdom of the Universe.

'When you make the two one, and when you make the inside like the outside and the outside like the inside, and the above like the below, and when you make the male and female one and the same......then you will enter the Kingdom'.

Jesus, from The Gospel of Thomas.

WHAT IS LIFE?

Why is there misfortune, misery and death?

Perhaps they are 'koans' to see how we cope. If you survive without too much anger and bitterness, then you are fit for heaven, i.e. they are a test, an examination.

Expanding the 'school' theory, they teach us about ourselves, as do any extreme circumstances. Maybe life is an Outward Bound course.

Then there is the concept of Satan's Fall, blighting God's perfect creation. Thus began the cosmic struggle between good and evil and a world of tension and antagonism in balance. Whether evil can create or simulate beauty to beguile and mislead us is one for the philosophers or the paranoid. Apart from the Bible declaring God will be the eventual winner, all flowers are the end product of decay. The worst of days can end with the most gorgeous sunset. A baby will always melt our hearts and bring out the best in us. And the sun always shines beyond the clouds. In other words, there is also much joy in life and there are grounds for optimism.

Without the emotive concepts of heaven, hell, God and the Devil, there are only positive and negative forces. Only our minds make them good and bad. Both are necessary for the Universe to function; everything flows and operates in rhythms, vibrations and waves or cycles. There is only energy and cause and effect; nothing is vindictive. However, what one person does to another may certainly be seen as good or bad and so such a theory must take into account fairness, justice and human rights. Anyway, much human misery is down to man, not supernatural forces, whether it is faulty technology or the way we treat the environment and each other.

Whether troubles are 'sent' by God or a Devil, is largely irrelevant, because all the 'maybe's' apply in any case. What matters is whether our attitude and thought-patterns are worthy of heaven.

We may meet it all serenely or express our feelings in the strongest terms to restore the emotional balance, depending on our make-up. But if you meet life with 'faith', or an attitude that, despite all appearances, all will be well, you are not only virtually untouchable but you deserve heaven. Good thoughts attract good things and in the long run, life tends to give us what we deserve.

'Nothing can harm a good man either in life or in death'.

Socrates.

BEYOND THOUGHT

The trouble with Thought is it thinks too much. It is the curse of the human race, a good servant but a bad master. It needs putting in its place. Only then may we gain access to our quintessential Self; only then can the Divine shine through.

So how can we create the circumstances for this to happen. How can we co-operate with the Tao? By using age-old psychological and spiritual devices to circumvent the thought-devil.

Such as:

* Controlled breathing, as in Yoga and Rebirthing.

* Stillness and relaxation, as in Meditation and Hypnotherapy.

* Meditation, as in T.M.

* Visualisation and guided imagery, as in Psychosynthesis, Dream work, Art work and Hypnotherapy.

* Chanting and other sound techniques.

* Special exercise disciplines, as in Yoga and Tai Chi.

* Body awareness methods, as in Massage, Bio-energetics, Float chambers, Alexander technique, etc.

* Emotional catharsis approaches, as in Co-counselling, Radical Hypnotherapy, Reichian therapy, Psychosynthesis, etc.

and many others.

But always with a reputable, experienced guide, teacher or therapist, and/or within a supporting framework.

TRUST AND FAITH

Assuming a premise that the Universe is benign and personal, why are we adrift on a sea of doubt, fear, despair, insecurity and defensiveness?

The first essential is to accept and believe it, i.e. trust that all is well, despite appearances - which may mean disbelieving the evidence of our eyes. Not easy for ingrained cynicism.

Only then will we begin to see. Only then will truth reveal itself.

A positive outlook engenders a positive response. That is the way the Universe works.

Trusting implies relaxation, for all will be well. Conversely, relaxation induces trust and positivity.

As change is one of life's absolutes, our philosophy must embrace it. We must let go and know that Goodness will come our way if our minds are tuned and responsive to it.

Life will happen without our striving. Our task is to recognise and appropriate our unique opportunities, yet know when to be open to the next one. We must move as lightly as possible through life, never grasping or become obsessed.

'We are not human beings on a spiritual journey.
We are spiritual beings on a human journey'.

Anonymous.

WE ARE WHAT WE EAT

It is obvious that if we abuse our bodies nutritionally we get what we deserve. In terms of both quantity and quality, the consequences of starvation or obesity can be dire. If we lack variety or balance in our diet, then there can be detrimental consequences.

Just as our digestive system urgently seeks food to devour, so we need sustenance on other levels. Our curious minds seek both knowledge and entertainment; knowledge can mean power and survival and entertainment diverts us from the difficulties if living.

At a higher level, many of us need spiritual succour. Not everyone realises they have this need, either because they are still preoccupied or dazzled by the world; because they have never been desperate enough to cry for help; or because they have never seen what is possible.

But for some, it is a yearning and a thirst, an essential need. We need to connect to a higher energy, to recharge our batteries. We need wisdom, peace, hope, joy, love, purpose.

It may be escape to wild places for silence and beauty to permeate the soul.

The serenity of relaxation, visualisation and meditation.

The companionship and comfort of a church, mosque, synagogue or temple.

The clarification of personal development and awareness groups.

The exhilaration and community of dance and music.

Giving effective help to those in need.

..........there are many means of soul-nourishment.

Sadly, a majority of humans beings seem content to rush around to clubs and parties, seek a bigger or better house or car, indulge their appetites to excess or seek the next thrill or trend, rather than learn, grow into awareness and give something back.

But the law is that, whether we feed on the positive or the negative at whatever level, what we consume determines what we become and our destiny.

'Man shall not live by bread alone.......'
The New Testament

REST

is a commodity in short supply, for various reasons. The modern world should have given us more time for rest, yet we fill it with more activity, as if we feel either guilty or afraid of stopping; afraid of Being, rather than Doing.

The Rat-race seems to regard it as weakness, the Church as sloth and the medical profession as unhealthy. Granted there are situations when mobilisation is preferable to stasis and a change is as good as a rest. True also that healthy excercise can maintain fitness: yet even this can become addictive, so it must be balanced by acivities which rest the whole personality. That means body, mind, emotions and spirit.

Medically, rest was once nature's biggest ally. The passive approach was the mainstay and convalescent funds and homes were common. Now, rest is almost wimpish in our hyperactive society. Besides, rest is deemed unnecessary when magic pills and clever surgery get us back on our feet in no time. Patient turnover rises and rises: greater and greater efficiency, more and more stress, less and less rest, more and more illness. Crazy , isn't it?

In fact there is not time in this super-industrial society for either body or spirit to recuperate, or even to be acknowledged. Little wonder that there are so many immune defficiencies, mystery ailments and chronic fatigue - or should it be chronic unrealised tension?

Rest in its total sense means not only a body that is reasonably fit and a body that is recharged by adequate sleep, not only a mind that is diverted and stimulated in an atmosphere that is only as challenging as we choose, but an emotional state that is guilt-free, spontaneous, joyful and as fulfilled as possible.

When these conditions are made possible, real vitality and exhilaration will follow and we may begin to appreciate life for the first time. We are talking of nothing less than spiritual liberation.

Holistic therapies can play a major part in this process.

'Quiet minds cannot be perplexed or frightened, but go on in fortune or misfortune, like the ticking of a clock in a thunderstorm'.

Robert Louis Stevenson.

STILLNESS

is the greatest need of the Human race, if we knew it.

The vast majority of us do not realise what stillness is, so geared are we to frenetic activity in the modern world. Stillness is almost painful to us. Fortunately, it is a habit that can be developed.

Stillness of body is a consequence of quietness of mind. This is the hardest part: to hear and still the ceaseless, chattering, everyday mind that goes round in circles - the 'monkey mind' of Buddhism.

We are fearful of nothingness if we achieve such stillness; the surprise is that potent images and words of wisdom begin to manifest as we wait in stillness. Some guidance may be needed in their interpretation, although we may intuitively recognise our own truths and what is right for us; we are our own experts.

We realise with awe and relief that we can indeed rely on inner strength, higher mind, an inner healer, greater wisdom, a spiritual dimension. Whether it be natural or supernatural.

Below the hectic surface.

At the hub of our Being.

'Breathe through the heats of our desire
Thy coolness and thy balm
Let sense be dumb, let flesh retire,
Speak through the earthquake, wind and fire
O still small voice of calm.'

J. G. Whittier

THE SPIRITUAL

The concept of Spirituality is not easy to define. It is anything which causes our Spirit to kindle, to come alive, to grow, to soar and sing. Anything which causes us to love life, to wonder, to have humility, to be grateful, to worship, to feel connected to an energy which transcends this world.

The opposites of Spirituality, of being fully aware, of being truly alive, are dormancy, deterioration and death.

We can choose to go one way or the other - either to stagnate (or rather deteriorate, for it is impossible to stand still) or to embrace the chance to put our feet on the road to Spirituality and thus realise our latent spark of Divinity.

Through an open but not gullible mind, a heart that allows itself to be just a little adventurous and romantic, a will that shows humility, courage and a certain faith, magic and miracles will guide us to unexpected spiritual fruits and our Divine heritage and goal - peace, truth, Wisdom, joy and love.

'Joy is consciousness. Life is to be enjoyed, to be made conscious by enjoying it. When you enjoy doing anything, you are conscious. Enjoy every moment of your life, and you're living joyously.

Joy or consciousness is your natural state. It's always there. It's like the sun, always shining above the shadow of the earth. Stop living in your own shadow and the sun, the joy, immediately shines.

To find joy nothing positive can be done. It's the practice of negation, shedding the shadow, that does it.

Living joyously is the joy of clarity - no problems. My whole life is then a joy or clarity of being - a being of joy and clarity. This is there now, inside you, just waiting to be lived. You don't have to strive for it, search for it or make it. It's you, it's yours, your very being'.

Barry Long.

SPIRIT

All form is illusion: it manifests and it fades or changes; although it may be allegorical, giving a clue to something less transitory. Consequently, the visual world - and mortal life - are illusions.

There are dimensions beyond the obvious. Those who make the effort to take time out and seek, develop awareness rather than consciousness, discovering realms and riches that surprise them.

For in silence and stillness, and with techniques that calm our ceaseless thoughts, other aspects of mind and soul manifest. We see with the eye and wisdom of the Spirit. We learn about ourselves: that our true nature is God-given and God-like.

'The body is always in time, the spirit is always timeless and the psyche is an amphibious creature compelled by the laws of man's being to associate itself to some extent with its body, but capable, if it so desires, of experiencing and being identified with its spirit and, through its spirit, with the Divine Ground'.

Aldous Huxley,

LEVELS, LOGIC, MAGIC

Creation/the Universe has many aspects/layers/levels/modes.
The microcosm and the macrocosm. The sub-conscious, the conscious and the super-conscious. The practical and the theoretical. The physical, the psychological, the spiritual. The material and the philosophical. The logical and the magical.

The logical is necessary to our physical, material, practical mode of everyday living. It helps us earn a living. Socially it helps ensure fairness and justice. It helps us understand the world and dispel superstitious excesses. It seems to occupy a middle level in the scheme of things.

But the logical can also shackle and blind us. Newton's mechanistic laws of the clockwork universe can not explain the microcosmic world of sub-atomic physics. Neither is it much help in inspiring our despair, or explaining our need for connection to a greater power. God for instance can never be apprehended or comprehended through logic. There are worlds beyond; levels of existence which transcend the material and the logical. The basic logic there says 'what you sow you reap'.

This is on the one hand frustrating and depressing; on the other, a reason for hope and liberation.

But what is the relevance to our lives?

It means appearances can be deceptive.
It means co-incidence can be meaningful and significant.
It means prayer can work.
It means magic and miracles can happen.
It means that God is in control and can override.
It means misery and despair will eventually be seen in perspective.
It is said that after death the first reaction is often laughter.
a) at relief that 'all is well'.
b) At the irony that our logical blindness ever doubted that it would be so.
It means that death is no big deal, but a natural and necessary transition and transformation.

'In studying the Perennial Philosophy, we can begin either at the bottom with practice and morality; at the top with consideration of the metaphysical truths; or in the middle at the focal point, where mind and matter, action and thought have their meeting place'.

Aldous Huxley.

MAGIC

What is lacking in this often ruthless, dark, senseless, monotonous world is magic.

Positive magic can enliven, enlighten, change and enhance everything. All things are possible when we discover and create the right conditions.

Magic has always existed; in fact it was far more common before we over-developed right-brain rationality at the expense of intuition, imagination and sensitivity. Miracles were certainly prominent in the days of early Christianity, indeed may have been the prime reason for its growth.

Christ inspired latent 'magical' abilities, which are inherent, rather than abnormal or supernormal; such spontaneity was replaced by the early church with ritual and dogma, because everyone being a magician threatened the hierarchy.

No doubt there is negative magic, which can do great harm. But those who pursue positive magic with the right motives will never be harmed. If we live with the Buddhist 'right thought, right will and right action', we demonstrate that intentions are good and our hearts humble and pure; these are the criteria which are likely to inherit the Kingdom.

Magic operates on many levels; God moves in mysterious ways. Science, or at least physics, is magic. Love is magic. Holistic or spiritual healing is magic; unexplained improvements do happen. Intuition is magic. Clairvoyance is magic. 'Just knowing' and turning up on someone's doorstep when they need you is magic. Dreams which foretell danger are magic. Finding self-esteem and joy and ending depression is magic. De-fusing anger is magic. Beneficial personality change and growth of the soul is magic. Unexpected financial help which saves a charity at the last minute is magic. Co-incidence can be magic. Creativity is magic. Caring is magic. Being born again is magic. Enlightenment is magic. Awareness is magic.

Just as atomic power exists in inert matter, so magic dwells in the substance of our souls.

'All things are possible to them that believe.'
Jesus.

THE CONDITIONS

For joy to be possible in our souls and magic to be normal in our lives, we must

a) 'Love' ourselves. It is always assumed that human beings have black, evil, greedy souls. Because for various reasons we do sometimes display such unfortunate qualities, it must not be forgotten that we are also capable of great good and great sacrifice. Perhaps loving ourselves is not the right word, but we should certainly not hate ourselves, as many people do consciously or otherwise. We should always strive to live to be able to respect ourselves and have justified self-esteem. Without it, we can not 'love' our neighbour; we are exhorted in the Bible to 'love our neighbour as ourselves'. So a good relationship with ourself - and therefore with our fellow man - is the basis for joy and magic.

b) Tied in with this is a need to embark on exploration of our emotions and our motives, Doing so helps to identify our prejudices and fears, both of which make impossible the openess of mind and trust which are necessary

c) An open and receptive mind, but not a gullible one. Intuitively you will know when an activity is right for you, but your rational mind should be on guard. It should also guard against irrational cynicism.

d) Relaxation, a form of trust, also appears to speed the process. When prejudices and fears vanish, receptivity is increased.

e) Taking time out is essential. For yourself with perhaps a daily short spiritual practice or a walk in the wilderness. But also in a group periodically, whether meditation, dance or personal development. Groups can magnify spiritual power.

f) In conclusion, our personal attitudes and motives determine how far we progress spiritually. It is for those who genuinely, humbly and persistently seek to strive and serve.

The Universe can not be fooled.

From the unreal lead me to the real.
From darkness lead me to life,
From death lead me to immortality.

Brihad-anranyaka Upanishad.

PRAYER

Does prayer work? Strange how we tend to resort to it in dire circumstances, even if it is just bargaining with the powers-that-be. Perhaps it really is a basic need.

Some fortunate souls can pray naturally and readily, as to a relative or friend. Yet with most of us regular prayer, if we can find something to say, can seem like talking to ourselves.

Prayer has various aspects; formal and informal, individual or collective, spontaneous or planned, talking and listening. In the end it is listening that matters, for many people find that if we create the conditions to truly listen, then answers come, although not always in the form we expect.

For one thing, the answers may be in symbols, not words, which is why certain methods of divination can be akin to prayer. For another the reply may be in one of three forms - yes, no or wait. Certainly be careful how you phrase your requests; 'Lead me to the other side of the desert of life' may mean life will be a desert for you. Our requests should be positive and not too self-centred; we should ask how we can help God.

Many people gain benefit from Meditation, which is akin to prayer because it is a listening or perceptive state.

Prayer is based on the concept of levels of superconscious awareness beyond everyday logic. These ideas were expressed by Carl Jung in terms of the collective unconscious and synchronicity, or meaningful co-incidence. At this level the rational can be by-passed and the apparently miraculous may occur. James Redfield also refers to such magical co-incidence in his books.

How it works is not clear, but we need to create the right milieu for prayer and use it with the right attitude. In the case of such methods as the 'I Ching' it is also necessary to ask the right questions.

The results can be surprising, as many will testify.

'.....grant me the serenity to accept the things I can not change, courage to change the things I can; and the wisdom to know the difference'

Reinhold Niebuhr.

Lord make me an instrument of your peace

Where there is hatred......let me sow love

Where there is injury....pardon

Where there is discord.....unity

Where there is doubt....faith

Where there is despair...hope

Where there is sadness....joy

Where there is darkness.....light

St. Francis of Assissi.

JOY AND SUNSHINE

So how do we live positively and joyously? Not by doing anything. Not by striving, but by simply being.

Carl Jung maintained that we need to recognise and integrate the negative or 'shadow' side of our nature rather than ignore or fear it.

Similarly, Barry Long says that discovering our natural joy is simply a process of negation, of shedding the shadow, not gaining, adding or striving for anything. It is coming out of the shadow into the sunshine.

Anthony de Mello's constant theme is that when we drop our obsessions, fears and illusions, then awareness, a fuller consciousness, a coming alive to heightened quality of life, will automatically ensue.

Those who have have been privileged to fall in love may remember the way life looked and felt so different and more wonderful.

A similar experience on a higher, spiritual level, is possible.

' Sell your cleverness and buy bewilderment;'
Cleverness is mere opinion, bewilderment is intuition'.

Jalaluddin Rumi, Moslem mystic.

AFTERWARDS

Afterwards, we will wonder why we ever doubted. As our perspective shifts, asking questions will seem irrelevant. It will all fall into place, as the last piece in a jig saw makes sense of the whole.

It will be a case of 'Why didn't I see that then; it is so obvious now'.

Fear will seem stupid, guilt irrelevant and revenge pointless. Although karma is likely to ensure justice.

There may be regrets as our progress is reviewed, but they will be put in perspective and the way forward will be clear.

We will feel immersed in an atmosphere of comfort, support, understanding and love. All will be well.

'We shall not cease from exploration
and the end of all our exploring
will be to arrive where we started
and know the place for the first time'.

T. S. Elliot

JESUS

Why exactly did Jesus come to Earth?

The traditional doctrine of blood sacrifice does not inspire, although many have embraced it through fear, guilt or gratitude. Neither does the standard funeral service offer comfort, with its emphasis on resurrection of the body, damnation and salvation.

The human race for whatever reason has become estranged from God. As the moon gets its light from the sun, so our faces are turned away from Him/Her. Thus our souls are not illuminated; literally un-enlightened.

Jesus came to re-kindle our Divine spark, to shed light on our darkness. To inspire. To humble us. To break down our defensiveness. To sensitise our hard shells so that we become responsive and regain our humanity. So that we come alive and regain awareness of our spirituality. This happens when we truly love what he embodied. But perhaps the most powerful and practical interpretation is that he came to identify and empathise with the human situation, so that he could never again be seen as distant and detached.

His birth was heralded with Joy and he promised peace and harmony.

The theologians have constructed a theory of blood sacrifice of God's son so that a cosmic ransom is paid, thus expunging original sin. For God could not condemn the world if it produced one blameless man. It may be that this legal device was theoretically necessary, although it is not clear how a physical mechanism can atone for a spiritual matter. However it can certainly be a powerful psychological device.

But this doctrine involves fear and guilt, which is no way to build a relationship.

In fact, Jesus' ultimate messages and his example were positive. He came to raise the level of our consciousness and expand our awareness. In a psycho-spiritual sense, he came to transmute our base metal into gold. But early in the Christian era magic, miracles and Joy were all but extinguished for political and psychological reasons.

Perhaps supremely, he bequeathed to us His Spirit.

'O Light that followest all my way
I yield my flickering torch to thee;
My heart restores its borrowed ray,
That in thy sunshine's blaze its day
May brighter, fairer be'.

George Matheson.

SALVATION

It can not be denied that the human race murdered Jesus, who was good, wise and humble, who preached peace, healed people and worked miracles. If Jesus didn't come to save us from sin by shedding his blood, thus paying a ransom (to God) to redeem our souls, then what is salvation and why the Cross?

The Cross says, 'I am capable of doing this to him. he lived and died.' To stop us in our clever, pompous yet despairing tracks. To awaken the good in us. To say 'God does not want you to dwell in self-centred darkness, you were not born for that; turn your eyes to my Light. Love me and my ways and your hard shell will break. Follow my example of simplicity and service for God's sake to find joy in your hearts, for the Kingdom of Heaven is within you. Let your soul awake; become aware of the way you are and what is possible. I will deliver you from ignorance and despair and give you joy, light and hope.

He came to raise our sights above and beyond the gutter and our narrow horizons. He came to say 'You have reason to respect yourselves, for you have Divine inheritance and the Kingdom of Heaven is within you'. He came to show us the potential of our true glorious nature.

He came to lift our heads and our spirits, to kindle our dormant divinity. To inspire our souls. To show us our blindness. To enlighten us, in the sense of lifting our burden of despair and in the sense of giving us eyes to see the truth. To turn our faces to light and love.

He came to make us realise that another level of living is possible if we yearn for his philosophy and change the world by living it. He lived, loved and died to identify with us; to say 'You are worth identifying with. Now I appreciate what it is to be human. Embrace my spirit and you can know what it is to be a truly spiritual being. Heaven and earth are one'.

If we thus uncover the Truth within us, not only will we have heaven in our hearts, we will accelerate its spread on earth.

'O love that will not let me go
I rest my weary soul in thee
And give thee back the life I owe
That in thine ocean depths its flow
May richer, fuller be'.

George Matheson.

CHRIST SPIRIT

The Christ Spirit has always existed. Always there have been enlightened souls and societies who instinctively knew more of the Truth than others.

His physical manifestation galvanised the world, with only the weapons of wisdom and love.

When he died, his words and His Spirit were interpreted through the imperfect and sometimes egotistical minds of men, causing distortion and often fatal division. Yet that Spirit is not confined to Christianity; it can be evident in followers of all persuasions and of none.

He said he would come again. That not only were there 'many mansions' in his Father's house but that this life and this world were of such import in the scheme of things that he would one day rule supreme in the heart of humanity.

Yet his second coming will be different, for the consciousness of man has irrevocably changed. The Spirit is working to make the ground of humanity fertile for the Christ to shine.

Now He will enhance the quality of our lives immeasurably (impart abundant and eternal life) by uniting us with ourSelves (our soul or Higher self), thus rejoining us (re-ligion) with the Father (at-onement).

The Way is through listening to the Universe, connecting with Self and networking with others, thus enabling Humanity to come together to express the Spirit through wisdom, inspiration, intuition and Love.

Spread the Light.

'The world as we know it is coming to an end. The world as the centre of the Universe, the world divided from the heavens, the world bounded by horizons in which love is reserved for the members of the in-group; that is the world that is passing away. Apocalypse does not point to a fiery armageddon, but to the fact that out ignorance and complacency are coming to an end'.

Joseph Campbell.

WHOLENESS AND UNITY

We may have been created individual and separate, but we can not exist in isolation, physically, psychologically or spiritually.

As human beings, beneath our veneers of culture, upbringing and skin colour, we have the same needs fears and joys. We are dependent on each other and on our environment. At this level, there is an inter-relatedness, not only with each other but also between the planet and the creatures it supports.

The eco-system of Earth is amazingly sensitive and balanced, resembling an intelligent entity. Everything is inter-dependent, from the smallest to the highest and we are an integral part of the whole. There is also much we do not yet know and we do not tread carefully enough in areas of which we are largely ignorant.

Unfortunately, the false separateness we feel breeds fear and self-pity and the first consequence of this isolated defensiveness is breadth of vision.

We do not properly appreciate the links between body, intellect, emotions and spirit. We are not sufficiently skilled in relating to each other. And we fail to see the greater whole and how we can harmoniously interact with this intelligent, responsive Universe. In the words of Buzz Aldrin, Astronaut, 'The human race is in virtual mutiny to the order of the Universe'.

'A minute's silence each day, observed by all mankind, would make an incalculable contribution to the planetary healing and balancing that are now so urgently required.

An entire day of silence, prayer, contemplation and fasting would work wonders'.

The Acorn Books.

THE BOTTOM LINE

This has been a selfish century, or rather a century of liberation of the self. Until now, individuals have been controlled by Princes and dictators, the Church, the State and various Institutions; not to mention poverty and disease.

We have gone some way towards alleviating the last two. We have devised a degree of democracy. Generally we have more money and leisure. We have jettisoned the type of religion which caused unspeakable horrors - thank God. People-power has largely overthrown experiments in socio-political philosophy which killed millions. We may yet see through the blind 'enlightenment' of science, which causes as much havoc as it cures.

But the liberated self that we have found is basically frightened by its freedom. It stumbles about aimlessly, because it it not aware that it has Higher counterparts waiting to be discovered and utilised.

The lower self, being asleep, blind, 'dead', rarely realises how unhappy it is. For all its new-found freedom, it does not have joy or peace or security. Consequently it resembles a loose canon. But it needed to be liberated, with all the risks that that entailed, to have a chance of realising that it has a Higher Self.

The Higher Self is the answer to our needs, hopes and dreams. When it is recognised, we come alive. And this happens when we look inside our amazing Selves (where better to hide the secret), using the means that this book has striven to indicate and reveal.

In the 1950s, avant-guard theologians were asserting that the 'second coming' would not be a physical manifestation, but the development of a higher consciousness in mankind; in effect the next step in evolution. It appears the Millennium is seeing the realisation of this insight.

'I believe that the world-view implied by modern physics is inconsistent with our present society, which does not reflect the harmonious inter-relatedness we observe in nature. To achieve such a state of dynamic balance, a radically different social and economic structure would be needed: a cultural revolution in the true sense of the word.

The survival of our whole civilisation may depend on whether we can bring about such a change. It will depend ultimately on our ability to adopt some of the Yin attitudes of Eastern mysticism; to experience the wholeness of nature and the art of living in harmony with it'.

Fritz Capra, 'The Tao of Physics'

POSTSCRIPT

We can not approach or even look at the sun, but its rays and its influence are essential to our lives and well-being. We can not know God, but we can gain immensely from opening ourselves to Him/Her.

Even Jesus knew despair, but most of the time I am persuaded, I intuit, I feel, I know, that all must fall into perspective. Light will prevail.

Simplistic perhaps, but indisputable - the sun does always shine beyond the clouds.

All will be well.

'In order that the mind
should see the light
instead of darkness, so
the entire soul must be
turned away from this
changing world, until its
eye can learn to
contemplate reality and
that supreme splendour
which we have called the
Good. Hence there may well
be an art, whose aim would
be to effect this very
thing'.

Socrates.

RESOURCES:

WAYS AND MEANS TO FULLNESS OF LIFE.

'The Means Exist......'

Complementary approaches to Health and Wholeness.

At the end of this Directory will be found a list of publications carrying addresses of organisations and individual practitioners in many of the therapies and techniques mentioned here. Other sources of information may be found in complementary health stores and alternative book and gift shops, and often local papers and phone directories.

Do not be too gullible, but give any approach you try a fair chance. If you find it beneficial and it works for you, that is all that matters.

Alexander Technique

Based on the idea that we have lost our natural relationship with gravity, this method uses kinaesthetic, non-verbal re-education to encourage better modes of posture and movement. In the process, there may also be altered states of consciousness and personality insights.

Aromatherapy

Based on the effects of essential oils on the body and nervous system, this is a rapidly expanding area. The oils, which may be derived from flower, fruit or wood, can be soothing, invigorating or sensual. They can be used as an incense, in a bath or by massage. Their effects are via the senses and nervous system on the mind and body generally: the nose is a very sensitive area and is adjacent to the parts of the brain dealing with emotion.

Assertiveness Training

A system of group therapy which acknowledges that we all have basic human rights and that insisting on these rights provides the personal power that may be lacking in our lives. It teaches methods and skills which substitute assertiveness for aggression or passivity, enabling us to stand up for ourselves and use our personal power properly, whilst not infringing the rights of others. In the process, the individual takes stock of themselves and becomes more self-aware. Self esteem and self confidence are likely to be enhanced.

Aura-Soma

is said to work on all levels of being. Everything we are is an expression of ourselves at a soul level. Everything we are and experience in the present moment is an expression of everything we have been in the past, as well as what we may be in the future.

Through Aura-soma there is the opportunity to renew and recycle ourselves at our deepest level, enabling us to live our lives consciously, unfolding our potential and recognising the beauty within ourselves.

Info. including Aura-soma teachers nationally, Tel: 01507 533581.

Ayurvedic Medicine

Ayurvedic means 'knowledge of life'. It involves a variety of ancient Indian means to enhance well-being and possibly heal, including diet and lifestyle change, herbal medicine, massage and sound/voice techniques.

Bates Method.

Sees many eye problems as a breakdown of the normal inter-dependency between mind and body; it is therefore a non-medical approach, practiced world-wide. The problem may be an indicator of a pre-disposing mental/emotional disorder or simply the consequence of habitually failing to use the eyes properly. It is claimed to help difficulties ranging from squint to astigmatism, as well as some cases of headache/migraine.

Contact: Bates association of Great Britain, 11 Tarmount Lane, Shoreham by Sea, West Sussex, BN43 6RQ.

Biofeedback

Uses the technology of galvanic skin response. A hand held monitor, costing a few pounds, gives an audible tone which is an indicator of the state of the autonomic nervous system. This method claims that by linking this feedback tone to relaxation through awareness, the subject can learn to lower the tone and thus the rate of functioning of the body.

Bodywork and Bioenergetics

Founded by Reich and Lowen, these also are techniques which maintain that we physically lock chronic emotional pain into our bodies, resulting in tension and dis-ease. Their methods use pressure and manipulation to produce emotional and physical release.

Bowen Technique

A method of enabling the body to restore itself. Involves gentle moves on muscles and connective tissue using thumb and fingers. Allows the body to do the work, without imposing the will of the therapist on the client. Applicable to various injuries and also possibly to conditions as diverse as M.E., hay fever, migraine and asthma.

Chiropractice

Similar to Osteopathy in using manipulation of the spine, chiropractice is different in its philosophy. Based on the principle that there is a life energy flow in the body, which is in effect an innate intelligence. Dis-ease will result from blocking of this flow. Chiropractice seeks to free the flow.

Cranio-sacral Therapy

Developed as an early 20th cent. offshoot of Osteopathy. Not only about helping people to feel more at ease, but about resolving core problems and significantly enhancing their situation. Could involve freeing parts of the body unable to move, or helping to unravel people's emotional restrictions.

Therapists 'tune in' to the rhythm of the fluid and nerves in the spine and brain, to facilitate access to the core of an individuals being. This enables resonance with the energetic pattern of the individual and their spiritual essence. Emotional blocks and rigidity may thus be freed.

Dance (Natural Dance, Circle Dance or Sacred Dance).

Many of these traditional dances originated in Eastern Europe. They are all danced in circles: some are slow, others lively. They all seem to have the effect of raising peoples energies (as do many kinds of dancing) and either calming or stimulating the spirit, whilst at the same time bringing the group into a remarkable state of closeness and harmony. When combined with other approaches such as relaxation, meditation or visualisation, the spiritual effects can be quite powerful.

Dramatherapy and Psychodrama

With a trained therapist, drama and role-play can provide opportunities to face, model and rehearse situations which cause us difficulties in life. In doing so, aspects of the personality can be liberated and developed so that the individual can become more integrated.

Dreamwork and Creative Workbook

Both of these involve keeping of a detailed journal or diary which can give powerful insights into the mind and personality

Encounter Groups, Sensitivity Training, Personal Development

Stimulated by the work of Carl Rogers in the 60s, groups were encouraged to come together to explore various methods of self-awareness, personal growth and interpersonal relationships. Many businesses now send their employees on these courses. Groups have one or more leaders, who may facilitate in a gentle, supportive manner or in a more confrontative way. Either way, the participants are likely to learn something about themselves, often enhancing their whole attitude to life.

Feldenkrais Method

These are techniques developed by a scientist called Moshe Feldenkrais after he was badly injured. All exercises are done lying on the floor and consist of gentle movements combined with raising mental awareness of what is going on in the body . The client is encouraged to find the optimum position or a better way of performing a movement. The net result is often a greater feeling of all-round well-being.

Gestalt Therapy

Developed in the 1950s by Fritz Perls, Gestalt is practised on individual or group basis. It seeks to make the individual aware of gaps in various parts of their personality - posture, communication, emotional barriers - in order to enable them to become more aware and more whole. It does this by concentrating on the characteristics of the personality here-and-now, rather than what happened in the past. It uses a variety of potent and practical techniques, including dreamwork,

A branch of psychology with potent practical applications, it maintains that life is always trying to grow towards wholeness and completion. Gaps and fragmentation cause pressure and dysfunction in the personality. Also life is constantly dividing between background and foreground. Parts of our personality we have denied whilst growing up need to be brought into the foreground, so that our being can become whole and complete.

Causes are not a prime consideration in Gestalt, which cleverly/effectively works with observed symptoms to produce results.

Guided Imagery

Relaxes the body via breathing techniques, then induces Alpha waves by Visualisation, thus calming the mind and increasing intuition, creativity and well-being. It is also used as a tool which may enhance the immune system and combat illness.

Hypnotherapy

Combines relaxation techniques with suggestion and visualisation to produce an altered state of consciousness which can facilitate the resolution of anxieties on a deep or superficial level, whether rooted in the past or anticipated in the future.

Kinesiology

Utilises the lines and points of energy as in acupuncture a) as a means of balancing and improving the body's natural energies b) as indicators of what is affecting you negatively, such as emotion, pain, food, stress, muscular or other imbalances c) as indicators of what treatments are required. Uses muscle testing as a diagnostic tool, treating the whole person, using a combination of gentle, safe techniques. Spans the full spectrum of health and healing, from its physical body application through nutritional health to psychotherapy.

Light and Colour Therapy

The therapeutic use of light and colour to create healing environments which work psychologically to create moods and beneficially affect mental balance and general health.

Massage: Therapeutic.

The most common and orthodox method is Swedish massage, designed to stimulate the blood and lymphatic systems to improve body nutrition via circulation and remove waste products. The side effect is close human contact which teaches us about self-awareness and can have beneficial effects on the emotions. Massage tends to have a cumulative effect.

Massage: Intuitive.

Employing a variety of techniques, the masseur uses the abilities of the right the brain to pick up signals from the subject intuitively, which may speed up whatever is being dealt with in the mind and body of the client i.e. the approach is to the whole person.

Massage: Community.

This involves people being taught in groups e.g. of friends or relatives, so that massage can become part of their lives, thus creating a permanent support network.

Meditation: Transcendental.

Originating in India, T.M. is now widely practiced in the West. It teaches a strict philosophical system and the central technique is internal repetition of a personal phrase or Mantra. Research has proved T.M. to be an effective meditation method. There is however a difference between meditation purely for relaxation as opposed to an inspirational technique.

Meditation: Buddhist.

There are many ways into this approach and many books on the subject. As with all techniques, the student should find their own best method.
There are now Buddhist groups in most areas

Metamorphic Technique

This technique is a gentle massage applied to the feet, hands and head, which aims to promote change and creative growth. Assumes that during pre-natal life, all our physical, mental, emotional and spiritual characteristics become established and energy blockages at this time influence our development. The practitioner acts as a catalyst, helping to improve energy flow and loosen blockages which hold us fixed in time, so that a metamorphosis of our way of living may occur

Neuro-linguistic Programming

Based on an analysis of the way we communicate and relate, NLP is essentially practical in providing skills to make these processes more effective. It changes the way we look at life and approach people. Doing so means that barriers between people are reduced and trust, confidence and relaxation occur much more readily. When communication and relationships are more effective, the individual can achieve more of their potential. These powerful techniques can be effective in many areas of life, from caring, education and business to hypnosis and counselling. In fact, anywhere where people deal with people.

Past-life Regression

Hypnotherapy has developed techniques which can take people back to face and resolve childhood trauma. A few therapists claim to take this further, to existences before birth. They maintain this can shed light on our circumstances in this life, enabling us to resolve or come to terms with them.

Peer Counselling

Also known as Co-counselling. A system of lay-counselling in which there are no experts such as psychiatrists or social workers. This system establishes networks or support groups of people who have completed a basic course in the principles of peer counselling. Each participant has equal power in the relationship because at the end of an agreed time they change roles and the counsellor becomes the subject of counselling.

The training course teaches methods which can help people to deal with emotional problems. Peer counselling is intended to be an on-going process, so that you have someone to turn to to off-load your feelings during the rough patches in life, thus clarifying the issues. It can be very effective.

Pilates

Is a programme of postural re-alignment and muscle re-education, the aim being greater flexibility and well-being. It can benefit repetitive strain injury, stress-related illnesses, food disorders, ME and back-pain. It is also used by dancers and sports people.

Psychosynthesis

Founded by Assagioli, this approach uses individual or group therapy to evoke inner imagery which can help the person understand themselves and thereby integrate the various parts and opposites in their personality. The consequence is less inner conflict and neurosis and greater fulfilment.

Primal Therapy

Based on the belief that emotional events during our development, when we were unable to deal with them properly, have chronic effects on our present personality. The therapy consists in taking the subject back to the causal event and allowing them to express the hurt cathartically. This technique is also employed in other therapies such as hypnosis and co-counselling.

Rebirthing

Based on a system of breathing, together with imagery and gentle manipulation, the aim is to re-enact the clients' birth process in the context of a small supportive group to produce beneficial personality change. On a superficial level it is relaxing: if emotional blocks are dealt with in the process, there is much greater sense of relief.

Underlying theory links developmental stages in the womb with spiritual development.

Rolfing

Ida Rolfe developed this technique, based on the concept that, during development, tension arising from faulty emotional responses becomes locked in the body, particularly the muscles, causing blocks and rigidity. We literally develop a hard shell. Rolfing seeks to redress this by a kind of forceful massage.

Reiki

An oriental word meaning 'universal life energy'. It is defined as being power which acts on and lives in all created matter. The term Reiki has been applied to a specific technique for restoring and balancing your natural life-force energy. A technique, which may be performed through the clothes, for harmonising energy and promoting well-being, physically, emotionally and spiritually.

Relaxation Techniques

Various methods can help induce a more relaxed state, including i) Differential Relaxation (tensing and un-tensing the muscles) and ii) Relaxation through Visualising parts of the body and calming situations. Particularly suitable for the more imaginative. Many book and audio tapes now teach these skills.

Sensory Isolation tanks (or flotation tanks).

By cutting off sensory stimulation, body and mind tend to unwind. These tanks are said to aid such relaxation. They are specially designed chambers, isolated from light and sound, containing a blood-heat solution which helps to neutralise the effects of gravity.

Sound and Voice Therapy

is based on the belief that there is dynamic power in sound and certain resonances and harmonies which can work to our benefit. Not only does music literally have its charms but the throat is a most potent source of expression, which is blocked to varying degree in most human beings.

Sound and voice are part of many eastern and western religious traditions and a few therapists have developed techniques which appear to be highly effective for enhancement of body-mind well-being. These may include communal humming or chanting and finding our own personal note which can have the effect of harmonising the frequencies of right and left brain hemispheres. Often combined with special breathing methods.

Shen

is said to be about emotional growth and empowering change. It is reputed to be a safe process that heals by unlocking trapped, painful emotion, whilst the client remains fully clothed. The certified Shen practitioner is skilled in reversing the effects of these pain-contractions, by directing the biofield or 'qui-energy', between their hands through your body, using techniques tested over years of clinical research.

Shiatsu

Like Acupuncture and Reiki, Shiatsu massage is based on Oriental principles of energy flow through the body. Where this is impeded, ill-health results.

Shiatsu massage is gentle manipulation to stretch the energy channels and improve the flow. It can be done through light clothes and a session takes about an hour. At the very least, the client feels extremely relaxed. Working intuitively, the therapist may identify a particular weak spot and recommend self-exercises.

Spiritual Healing

Described by Mathew Manning, one of Britain's best known healers as 'channelling some form of universal, unconditional love' into patients. Others compare the sick body to a car in need of the 'jump leads' of divine energy to restart the patients own healing process. It is applicable to all types of illness and can be effective, painless and without side effects. It is also very comforting.

Touch for Health

A self-help technique, combining muscle-testing, massage and acupressure. originated in a College of Nursing in America, and now widely used wherever 'tender loving care' is called for.

Tai Chi

This is an ancient oriental form of gentle exercise, still widely used in China and worldwide. It consists of a series of exercise patterns performed in slow motion. This has the effect of slowing down the participants, with several results. It makes people more aware of their movement, thus helping them to slow down their everyday lives: the consequence is that they are likely to be more in touch with the natural rhythms of life. A second effect is to enhance mental and physical balance, because slow movement requires considerable balance. Thirdly, these exercises require a fair amount of discipline. The overall effect is one of harmony and well-being.

Transactional Analysis

This is based on an original way of looking at the personality devised by Dr Eric Berne, who wrote 'The Games People Play'. T. A. maintains that we all have within us three mind states - parent, adult and child. The child may be well hidden but nevertheless it is present and there are times when it must be expressed. Different situations in life require a response from the appropriate part. In one day, we may use our parent, adult or child many times.

A second tenet of T.A is that people need these aspects of personality nurturing, whereas Society tends to base its relationships and communication between people more on 'put-downs', which damage the personality. The consequence is that people consciously or otherwise, play games with each other, some of which can be deadly.

Thirdly, we all tend to be set on a certain path in life - T. A. calls this a 'Life Script' - and courses in the subject enable us to take a hard look at our characteristic way of responding to others and how our life scripts may need changing.

Transpersonal Psychology

Originated by Jung, Maslow and Assagioli. Believes that human beings have great potential which needs realising and releasing. Its methods are esoteric, including imagery, fantasy and altered states of consciousness to put people in touch with their intuitive higher selves, thus increasing self-esteem, creativity and a sense of purpose and often a spiritual dimension to life.

Yoga

It is difficult to generalise here as Yoga has branched into so many aspects over 1000s of years. It is a system of breath and body exercise, discipline and control which can lead to physical relaxation, confidence and well-being. These are the first steps to peace of mind and spirit, which can be pursued through the philosophical aspects of the subject.

Zero Balancing

A form of manipulation that aims to balance out the body, mind and soul. Based on the concept that the body contains an invisible 'energy body', which can become kinked or twisted e.g. after an accident or emotional stress. The therapist will aim to harmonise energy lines through a manipulative 'dialogue' with the energy system.

Also various alternative approaches to maintaining the well-being of the whole person e.g. Osteopathy, Homeopathy,

Acupuncture, Acupressure, Reflexology and Zone Therapy, Bach Flower Remedies,

Information will be found on these subjects in book shops, libraries and the sources of information mentioned at the end of the Directory.

IMAGINE : A VISION

(Reprinted from Spirit of the Age Magazine)

IMAGINE..........

A centre/institute/temple/church in every town/district/ community.

With many rooms, some large, communal, inspirational; making use of beautiful structure, form, colour, light and sound.

Others small, individual, comfortable and therapeutic.

This concept/project/dream could have its essence expressed in a title, perhaps with a logo e.g. Centre for Healing, Relaxation, Inspiration, Spirituality and Truth.

The Centre for Development/Promotion of Relaxation, Intuition, Inspiration, Spiritual Renewal, Personal Growth, Human Potential.

The Spiritual Oasis.

The Halls of (Eternal/Constant) Light.

Its lights would shine and it would be open for anyone, as a drop in centre in part, 24 hours a day, 365 days a year.

There would be no dogma, no judgement and no compulsion or coercion. A recognition that everyone's path to the Source is individual.

"In My Father's House are many Mansions". There could be :

A Hall of Stillness, Colour and Light.

A Hall of Relaxing Music and Voice.

A Hall of Relaxing Words.

A Hall of Inspirational Words.

A Hall of Visualisation and Guided Imagery

A Hall of Movement and Dance.

A Hall of Massage or similar

Perhaps all this could be summed up as Passive/Active and Sound /Silence.

Furniture would be minimal. Shoes would be removed on entrance. To lie down in most halls would be encouraged, although allowance would be made for those less than mobile. The motto could be 'Drop in, Lie down, Tune in'.

Lying down for all passive activities would be recommended because the floor is :

Secure and safe

Supportive

Levelling (equality)

Humble

Relaxing

Real (in touch, grounded)

Lying supine encourages rest, non-aggression, openness and receptivity.

Responsible for each Hall/Dept/Faculty might be a Guide/Supervisor/Director, skilled in the arts practiced/experience offered there, and for its Programme of activities.

Each Hall could have satellite therapeutic rooms, so that the personal and spiritual insight gained in the main halls could be explored and consolidated.

There might also be an educational function to extend and deepen the activities and train helpers, guides and directors. The venture may eventually become something akin to a University of Spirituality and Human Potential. It might even eventually have its own radio/TV station.

Various dilemmas would need attention. What would be the composition and function of the governing Body. You would think that as the members would naturally be from fields related to personal development and interpersonal/transpersonal relationships, there would be few snags but human nature is not that simple. There might be many differences of approach to be ironed out and no doubt the requirements of European directives on Therapies would have to be tackled: this would surely be an opportunity to air these issues and raise the profile of the whole concept of the Centre.

Another sticking point might be the matter of when a person should be expected to take responsibility for themselves. This might be minimised if certain approaches which were either non-threatening or self-supportive, (or just plain enjoyable), were central and on-going, such as meditation, tai chi, feldenkrais, dance and community massage. A co-counselling type support system might underlie the whole concept. Others philosophies and therapies could be made available on a periodic tuition or short course basis e.g. Transactional analysis, Psychosynthesis.

A policy would have to be determined as to whether the Centre should have a social arm, also how to deal with social misfits and the mentally ill, as such a haven would no doubt attract them. In theory the Centre should have much to offer those suffering from anxiety, anger, depression and low self-esteem.

Then there is the question of finance. It would probably have to be voluntary , so that the Centre would be seen to be genuine and non-profit-making. People would be invited to contribute according to their means and the benefit they feel. Trust or Foundation status might be established and bequests and donations sought. Perhaps some ideas could be borrowed and lessons learned from Findhorn, Skyros, or similar holistic centres.

Simplistic? Far-fetched? Idealistic? And what is the matter anyway with the present commercial set-up regarding personal growth and self-awareness?

Maybe, but imagine - Humanity being offered the chance to stop the rat race and drop out into a Spiritual Health Service-type provision of support and non-judgement, even joy? A resource to allow us to Be, to grow, to renew our ability to face life and to liberate and permit expression of the joyful spiritual potential within every heart. Because not only common sense but all esoteric teachings say that that is where the future must start.

THE MEANS EXIST.........
"Seek and you shall find".

'By their fruits you shall know them'

It is incumbent upon the reader to find their own Path, keeping an open but not gullible mind, in order to differentiate between the genuine and false practitioner or teacher.

The following magazines and periodicals deal with Holistic Health, Spiritual and Environmental issues:

Caduceus Magazine, 38 Russell Terrace, Leamington Spa, Warwickshire.

Kindred Spirit Magazine, Foxhole, Dartington, Totnes, Devon. Tel: 01803 866686 www.kindredspirit.co.uk

Resurgence Magazine. Subs: Jeanette Gill, Rocksea Farmhouse, St Mabyn, Bodmin, Cornwall, PL30 3BR. Tel: 01208 841824. www.resurgence.org

Human Potential Magazine, 5 Barb Mews, Brook Green, London, W6 7PA. Tel 0171 371 2432.

Cygnus Bookclub, PO Box 15, Llandeilo, Carmarthenshire, SA19 6YX. Tel 01550 777701 www.cygnus-books.co.uk Email enquiries@cygnus-books.co.uk

Healing Today, the magazine of the National Federation of Spiritual Healers, Old Manor Farm Studio, Church St., Sunbury on Thames, Middlesex, TW16 6RG tel 01932 783164 www.nfsh.org.uk

The following organisations are also relevant, providing therapy, training or guidance:

The Institute for Complementary Therapies provides independent information about therapies and has a list of registered therapists. ICM, PO Box 194, London, SE16 7QZ. Tel: 020 7237 5175. Email icm@icmedicine.co.uk   www.icmedicine.co.uk

The National Federation of Spiritual Healers, Old Manor Farm studio, Church St., Sunbury on Thames, TW16 6RG. Tel: 01932 783164.

A COURSE IN MIRACLES, Foundation for Inner Peace, PO Box 635, Tiberon, California, 94920, USA.

The Barry Long Foundation, 7 Nichol Place, Cotford St. Luke, Taunton, TA4 1JD. Tel 01823 430061

Centre for Health, Healing and Self-development, Runnings Park, Croft Bank, West Malvern, Worcs., WR14 4DU. Tel 01684 573868. www.runningspark.co.uk

The Findhorn Foundation, The Park, Forres, IV36 0TZ Tel 03094 574547

Skyros Holistic Holidays, 92 Prince of Wales Rd., London, NW3 3NE Tel 0207 267 4424.   connect@skyros.com

The Quest, Home Study Programme in Personal and Spiritual Growth. Designed to re-discover a sense of the soul. Dept JG, PO Box 5369, Forres, IV36 3WG. Tel 01309 692115. Email: thequestproject@aol.com.

ACKNOWLEDGEMENTS

Grateful thanks for permission to use extracts are due to:

Random House Group Ltd. for extracts from The Perennial Philosophy by Aldous Huxley.

Barry Long Books for the passage from How to Live Joyously by Barry Long.

Piatkus Books for material from Stepping into the Magic by Gill Edwards.

Harpercollins Publishers Ltd. for extracts from Awareness by Anthony de Mello.

David Higham associates for passages from The Tao of Physics by F. Capra.

Bantam Press, a division of Transworld Publishers, a division of the Random House Group Ltd. (All rights reserved) for the extract from Mind to Mind by Betty Shine. Copyright 1989 by Betty shine.

Beacon Press, Boston for quotes from Dreaming the Dark, Copyright 1982, 1988, 1997 by Miriam Simos

Books to which I am indebted include:

Zen and the Art of Motorcycle Maintenance	Persig R
The Dancing Wuli Masters	Zukov G
The Aquarian Conspiracy	Ferguson M
Mind Over Body	Coleman V
Mind Gymnasium	Postle D
Mind Control	Silva J
Coming Alive	Proto L

Life Between Life	Whitton J and Fisher J
Psychology with a Soul	Hardy J
What We May Be	Ferrucci P
The Act of Will	Assagioli R
Stress and Self Awareness	Bond M
Learning Human Skills	Burnard P
Towards a Psychology of Being	Maslow A
The Acorn Series	Acorn Publishing
The Prophet	Gibran K
The Perennial Philosophy	Huxley A
A Father's Book of Wisdom	Jackson Brown H
The Faith of the Counsellors	Paul Halmos
The Battersea Park Road To Enlightment	Isobel Losada
The Spiritual Tourist	M Brown

Other reading which has contributed to the total picture:

The Tao of Chaos	Walter K
The Tao of Pooh	Hoff B
The New Summerhill	Neill A.S.
Future Shock	Tofler A
What is Psychotherapy?	Bloch S
Walden 2	Skinner B F

An Introduction to Jung's Psychology	Fordham
Living beyond Fear	Segal J
The Practice of Personal Transformation	Williams K
The Transparent Self	Jourard S.
Synchronicity	Jung C
Zen mind, Beginners Mind	Suzuki D T
The Four Loves	Lewis C S
Nice people or New Men	Phillips J.B.
Hypnosis	Hartland J
The Gnostics	Churton T
Alternative Medicine	Stanway A.
The Sensual Body	Liddell L
The Science of Living	Adler A
Gestalt Therapy	Perls F
Gestalt is	Sullivan (Ed.)
The Quantum Gods	Love J
Dibs: in Search of Self	Axline V
Zen and the Art of Caring	Brandon D
In and Out of the Garbage Pail	Perls F
The Teachings of Don Juan	Castenada C
The Healers Handbook	Reagan & Shapiro
New Age Handbook	Campbell & Brennan
Miracles on Demand (Hypnotherapy)	Tebbetts C.
Wholeness and the Implicate Order	Bohm D.

The Tao of Physics	Capra F
The Celestine Prophecy	Redfield J
Body Learning - An Introduction to the Alexander Technique	Gelb M.
Bioenergetics	Lowen A
Encounter Groups	Rogers C.
Gestalt Therapy Now	Fagan & Shepherd,
Massage & Meditation	Downing G
The T.M.Technique	Russell P
The Feeling Child	Janov A.
Rolfing - The Integration of Human Structures	Rolf I
Shiatzu	Irwin & Wagenvoord
Games People Play	Eric Berne
Yoga and Meditation	Hewitt J
Tranceformations	Bandler and Grindler
Frogs into Princes	Bandler and Grindler
Merlin the Immortal	Quiller P
The Seekers Guide: A New Age Resource Book.	Ed: John Button & William Bloom.

INDEX.
